At Last a Life and Beyond

Anxiety and Panic Free

By

Paul David

Acknowledgements

I would like to thank my mother for her help with all the proof-reading and for also being there for me in all my years of suffering and beyond. I also want to thank all the people who have recovered or are well on their way to recovery and now give up their free time to advise and help others through my blog and Facebook page.

Although I came to a lot of my own conclusions, throughout and beyond my suffering, I have been influenced by many different teachings and people, and although there are too many to mention here, they will always have my utmost respect and gratitude.

Contents

Copyright

ISBN 978-0-9569481-3-7 www.anxietynomore.co.uk

Foreword

How do I get rid of my anxiety?

I searched around many years for the answer to this question. I asked therapists, read numerous books, searched the internet, asked on forums and yet no one could give me the elusive answer to this question. The reason that no one could give me this answer is because the answer never existed.

What I found out after years of searching is that you cannot forcibly get rid of anxiety by actively doing something, in fact as many of you may have realised, the harder you try to get out of your anxious state, then the worse it gets. It is only by taking the opposite approach of doing nothing, that you can live a life free of suffering. Read on, and by the time you reach the end of the book, you will understand why.

Most of you reading this will more than likely have read my first book ***At Last a Life***. The initial book was written after my own struggle to find an answer to a condition which has now reached number one on the list of reasons why people visit their doctor. For something so common, there still seems to be limited help out there and so much conflicting advice. It pains me to see some of the advice handed out at times on a condition that is so misunderstood, making recovery seem so difficult and extremely confusing.

The initial book was written because I genuinely wanted to help people who feel like they are stuck on a merry go round of self-help while seemingly getting nowhere. I have personally known people who have spent 20 plus years in therapy; how can this ever be right? This is what I set out to change, as I too suffered for many years going from one treatment to another wondering if anything would ever help. Eventually, I'd had enough of the conventional therapy that brought me little to no relief and went off to seek my own answers. In my opinion, a lot of self-help is still stuck in the dark ages where digging up the past, taking pills or a new technique is considered to be the answer to all ills.

In this book, you won't find a list of techniques, rules or methods, as you don't need them. I am sure you have tried enough of these and still found little relief. This is where I think a lot of the so-called cures are flawed. Techniques, rules and methods usually require more effort and are mostly built around the suppression of thoughts and feelings, which is the completely wrong approach. Anxiety is your mind and body's way of telling you that you are already overdoing it with effort, both mentally and physically, so the last thing you want is to add more to an already overworked mind and body.

To recover from anxiety, we need to start taking away from the workload, not adding to it. We need to give the mind less to do, not more. If you ask anyone who has recovered, you will never hear them say "Well I have my sayings, techniques and rules to follow now and I am fine". No, they will say the complete opposite such as, "I no longer do this, and I no longer do that". The truth is you don't need to do anything; it is all the 'doing' and attempts at manipulating your current state that are actually keeping you in the loop of suffering.

I am now fully recovered and live a very full and peaceful life. The only difference in me now is I no longer overthink, no longer stress, no longer worry, no longer avoid, no longer spend all day going over things in my head and no longer exert immense mental energy trying to control or suppress my thoughts and feelings. I did not find some way to get rid of my suffering; I just stopped doing everything that was causing it. Recovery will not come through spending all your time playing mental games, suppressing or trying to master some new technique; all this will have the opposite effect.

Anxiety is self-created

Anxiety needs a creator and you have the power to create, it's nothing more than a self-created condition kept alive through a lack of understanding. There is no outside force doing this to you; there is no ***thing*** to be beaten or defeated here. We are unknowingly doing this to ourselves and are responsible for our own suffering.

You may be asking, 'Why write a book then if there is nothing to do?' In order to get to that stage of non-doing, I had to educate myself to understand why the previous things I had been doing hadn't worked. I had to see why these past behaviours were making me worse and how I was creating more of the very thing I was trying to get rid of. That ironically, the attempted cure had actually become the cause.

So, it was never about learning what to do; it was about learning what not to do. I began to understand that all my mind and body needed was for me to step out of the way and then the most intelligent system there is would start its own process of healing. The same system that would effortlessly heal me if I broke my arm or cut my finger was more than capable of healing me physiologically and emotionally too.

Through understanding, I developed an entirely new attitude where I could still feel anxious, have irrational thoughts and yet be totally detached from them. Without the fuel of fear, worry and obsession, I opened the door to recovery. Previously I had spent years attempting to control, suppress and avoid my feelings due to my hatred/fear of them. I would spend hours in my head, constantly worrying, fighting and analysing in an attempt to fix myself, then wondered why I felt so mentally worn out and detached from my surroundings. I finally realised that *I* was the only reason I was getting worse, not better.

Why did I decide to write a new book?

Well, the initial book was written all those years ago with little or no expectation, and although I really thought I had something to say, I never expected it to achieve the success it has. To see the reviews on Amazon and hear so many people telling me that their doctor or therapist has recommended it, is very humbling, and it is extremely satisfying that my words have been able to touch and help so many people.

It was due to this success that I started my blog, Twitter and Facebook page and through this, I learned that some people still seemed to misunderstand certain points or really struggled with particular issues that were maybe not covered the first time around. So, I wanted to address all of this, as my main concern is for people to reclaim their lives. I have also learnt a lot more over the last nine years, as you never stop learning or finding new ways to explain things. So, when I thought I had enough information for another book and new ways of getting my point across, I decided to start writing.

By the end of this book, you will have learnt why you have remained in a cycle, how the mind and body work, how you have unknowingly been creating a lot of your own anxiety and why what you have been doing so far has been counter-productive. When you recognise this, then trust me, this is the catalyst to no longer suffering.

A lot of people fail to realise that we are all born with a healthy default setting, one that we can move away from, but one we can never lose and a place we can all go back to once we learn to step out of our own way and allow a process of healing to occur. All the thoughts and emotions you currently feel are just surface symptoms and once they pass, you will realise that you are exactly the same underneath as you were previously. What you have been through causes no lasting physical or psychological damage and it has not harmed your natural well-being in any way.

This book was written solely by me, someone who was in such a dark place; a place from which I never thought I could recover. My list of symptoms would fill this book on its own. I could have seen out the rest of my years just getting by, not living a life but merely existing. But I was never happy with that and I did everything I could to find answers, not just for me but also to pass on to others, so they didn't have to suffer in the way I did. There truly is nothing more rewarding than someone coming back to you and telling you that they now have their life back.

The emails of thanks I receive on a weekly basis and the success stories that I have been sent inspires me to keep passing on what I know, and I have total confidence in the information I offer. So, all I ask is that you don't just read what I say, but trust in it and implement it. I always tell people I can pass on the information, but I cannot make you follow it. The real change has to come from you.

There may also be a need for you to go back to certain sections and reread them. People often tell me that once their knowledge and understanding grows, on reading the book the second time around, they see something that now truly makes sense and takes on a new meaning. This is the reason I may repeat the same message but explain it in a different way. On several occasions, I have explained something to someone in a slightly different way and they say 'Ah, right, now I get it'. When viewed from a different perspective, what I say can produce a real 'aha' moment. Hopefully, you will have plenty of these 'aha' moments as you read through this book. Nothing and I mean nothing, came close to helping me other than a better understanding of my condition. It took so much fear and wasted effort out of the equation. So much of recovery is not about doing something but more about seeing something, as when you truly see something for yourself, then the behaviour that has been causing you so much suffering automatically falls away.

A lot of the content will be relevant to your situation and some may not. I have just tried to cover the main questions that are asked of me on a regular basis. There are also some explanations that will hopefully help people in their everyday life too. I wanted to be able to take people beyond recovery, to give them the tools to recognise the damage caused by worry and stress and how they can live a life without it.

As I have covered the subject of anxiety and explained what it is in my first book, *At Last A Life*, I did not feel the need to go over that again. I wanted this book to be packed with help and advice about what is keeping you in the loop of suffering.

A lot of people who have read my first book have now fully recovered, but others, although they have made a lot of progress, still need a little more help to get to an advanced stage of understanding that will finally free them completely. Hopefully, this book will give you everything you need to take you over that final hurdle and answer any concerns you still have so that you can go back to living the life you desire.

I genuinely want to take you out of the self-help loop so you can finally begin to leave it behind and move on with your life, a life beyond your suffering.

That is why the title of this book is:

'At Last a Life and Beyond'

Chapter 1

You Are Not Broken

For years I believed and fell for the lie that I was broken, and with all the labels given to me through books, doctors and counsellors seeming to confirm this, I set off on a route of trying to fix myself by taking tablets, going back into my past and trying numerous techniques with the promise that they would 'fix' a broken me. I bought into it all and wasted a lot of time, money and effort. The truth is that I never was broken; I had lost my way and created a lot of my own suffering, yes, but I was never broken.

What I failed to realise is that I was the conductor of my own experience. I was the one continuing to create my anxiety and also the one keeping myself stuck. I did not need fixing at all. All I needed was to be told to stop doing the very things that were keeping me in the loop of anxiety, yet in many cases, I was told the opposite. I was given advice on how to suppress, manage and get rid of my anxiety and eventually realised that although certain people meant well, they were sending me in the completely wrong direction.

Following my recovery, I started to read up on Buddhism and other practices, as it has always been of interest to me to read different approaches on how the mind and body work. Having studied these practices and understanding the message behind them, I discovered that basically, they all say the same thing, but in different ways. Which is that in order to feel peace of mind and well-being, we must leave ourselves alone. We cannot force or create peace or well-being, and we won't find happiness by searching for something outside of ourselves. We all have perfect well-being, peace and happiness at core, and we are the only ones who can take ourselves away from it.

We are always being sold an image by the media that happiness comes from material things, from being a size 8, having the latest fashions, or the latest car or gadget. Consequently, people constantly try to find happiness outside of themselves when, in reality, true happiness always comes from the inside. The same is true for anxiety sufferers. The cure for anxiety is not on the outside, but on the inside, and once we sort out the inside, everything else just falls into place. We don't need to keep going around searching for things to make us feel at peace; we already have them. It is the very battle to find peace that takes us further away from it.

I looked back to when I recovered from anxiety and realised that this is the conclusion I eventually came to and passed on to others. The reason I got better was due to the fact that I just stopped doing all the things that had taken me away from my natural state. All the worrying, obsessing, stressing, overthinking, focusing is what took me away from the peace that was always present. When all this ceased through a process of understanding, then I slowly began to go back towards my natural state of being and the old me began to resurface.

Yet we are continually being told that we must do something about how we feel - fight it, suppress it or distract ourselves from it. But the only conclusion I came to in my days of suffering was that everything that helped me was a 'not do' and everything that made me feel worse was a 'do'. The more effort I put into trying to get better, the worse I felt, and the more I gave up trying, the better I felt. The reason is that you cannot think or battle yourself back to well-being; it happens naturally when you finally surrender to how you feel and end this inner battle you are having with yourself.

You may have seen an advert on the internet entitled 'How to eliminate anxiety'. Well, good luck with that one. I tried this for ten years and just got worse. Someone once said to me on my Facebook page "Paul I have been battling this now for 22 years and I won't stop until I beat it." I asked them if they had ever considered that after 22 years of nothing changing, then this may not be the way forward.

The point is, when we leave ourselves alone, we go back to our natural default setting. This setting is what we are all born with and it never leaves us. As the title says, 'you are not broken' so you don't need to run around desperately trying to fix yourself. If you leave yourself alone, then you will find everything you are looking for and realise that so much of your suffering came from your continued attempts to escape it.

I loved what someone said after reading a line out of my first book and telling others how this helped him to recover. Initially, I had said, "You do not need to search for recovery, rather let recovery come to you." He then said to others "If Paul says recovery will come to me, why am I wasting time trying to find it?" He truly understood the real meaning behind these words, which is that you can't find recovery through constant worry and effort.

People always want something to 'DO. They want an ABC technique; a method to recover. I am always hearing "What do I do?". This is a natural response in the mind. The mind says 'I don't like this, so find some way to get rid of it', and so we respond by struggling, fighting or trying some new technique to suppress. But again, this is not how recovery works. If it was, I am sure you would have come across this magic technique by now. You can't recover this way because anything you suppress just stays within your inner space and so you can never be free of it. There are many forms of suppression - distracting, avoiding, fighting - basically anything you do in an attempt to NOT feel an uncomfortable emotion is suppressing.

Some people make a lot of money out of promising to eliminate anxiety. They are everywhere, yet they have very little, if any, success, as you cannot eliminate something that is self-created. You just have to learn to stop creating it in order to cut off its fuel supply and then go through a process of healing.

The stress that first leads to anxiety can come from any number of reasons. Nobody wakes up and just feels anxious, so we initially created the anxiety. The anxiety we initially feel is just our mind and body's way of telling us that we are overworking them, like an inner alarm bell going off. It is sending us a message to slow down and not to stress and worry as much. Yet if you go on any anxiety forum, you will see so many posts saying things like 'I am really worried about this new feeling; I am scared of all these thoughts I have; I worry that I no longer feel any love for my husband'. Yet all that these worrisome thoughts do is create more anxiety and unpleasant emotions.

Also, the mental effort exerted trying to make sense of how they feel while trying to escape it only succeeds in draining them mentally and physically. Is it any wonder so many people stay in the cycle?

Your suffering is there for a reason. It is sending you a message that something is wrong, that what you are doing is not helping, that's its job. I recently explained this to someone who was having endless inner turmoil about her anxious thoughts and feelings and was constantly trying to do something about them. I asked her how this felt and she said that it was awful and made her feel worse. I said, "The problem is that you are constantly at war with what is arising through fear and resistance. This is your body's way of telling you to stop trying to resist, as these thoughts and feelings will come regardless. You trying to resist and deny them is causing more inner conflict and is the reason you feel all this extra discomfort. This extra suffering is just sending you a message that this is the wrong approach".

It was the same with me. When I fully allowed my thoughts and emotions, my body preferred this and told me so by creating less discomfort. When I tried to deny and suppress them, then I experienced far more internal chaos, which was my body's way of telling me that this was not the right path.

So, we have not only created the anxiety; we are the reason it continues to hang around. This is why the answer comes from the inside and never the outside. You are the one creating it, so you are the only one who can stop creating it and, trust me, nothing creates more anxiety than constantly fighting and resisting it.

Think of your brain as a computer because that is what it is. However, this computer did not come with a manual, so you don't always know what it is trying to tell you. But your computer is there to protect you in the best way it can and when you feel anxious, it is just doing its job and warning you that you are overdoing things and spending too much time indulging in worry and stress. If you fail to heed this warning and continue to add more stress and worry to the mix, it then starts to have an adverse effect on both your mind and body and you begin to feel mentally worn out and experience the effects of continuous anxiety. What people then tend to do is to worry and stress about their anxious state and so begin to sink deeper into the condition. This is sadly the cycle that so many people enter and the cycle I went through for so many years.

In the midst of my suffering, I used to spend hours and hours daily chewing on my so-called problems and then wondering why I felt like crap! Yet who was the one creating these horrible, negative feelings? - ME and ME only! There was no one else responsible for the way I felt, but me! Yet what did I blame it on? "Poor old me, look how I feel, this isn't fair". On and on I would go, stuck in more hours of negative, unproductive thinking, dragging my mood down even further and creating more stress, while continuing to believe that it was something outside of me that was creating the way I felt.

Your brain eventually ends up like an overworked computer that does not have enough space and memory to cope with all the worry and stress you are feeding into it, yet you expect it to work perfectly. All this worry, stress and overthinking can in some cases lead to poor mental health. The symptoms of this being a lack of sleep, feeling irritable and snappy, having no energy for routine tasks, difficulty remembering anything, lack of mental clarity and feeling the need for isolation. If this is you, then it is time to make some changes and give that poor brain the break It so desperately needs to regain its clarity and health.

I have explained this to people in the past and, ping, a few get it instantly, but some just go back to the worry state, thinking if they keep worrying and analysing enough, the elusive secret to free them of their suffering will magically appear. Trust me the last thing your mind needs now is more worry and stressful thinking. It is like dumping more trash on a rubbish dump each day and wondering why it isn't clearing.

It's incredible the wasted energy people put into trying not to feel something when all that energy could be saved by just allowing themselves to think and feel whatever arises. People are always asking me how they should go about no longer struggling, as the instinct to do so just seems automatic. I say, 'You don't actively try not to struggle; once you learn to be open to anything then there is no struggle'. It really is that simple. This letting go usually comes when they have run out of techniques and strategies and finally understand how much extra pain this struggle is causing them and how it is keeping them in the cycle of suffering.

A woman on my blog once stated that she struggled to get the subject of anxiety out of her mind. She found it near impossible to shake off this habit and be able to think and engage in other things. A response from another lady summed up what I am trying to say.

She said:

Once I completely unfollowed all anxiety related stuff online, stopped reading books on the subject, stopped discussing it with others and finally decided that I was going to enjoy my life with or without anxiety present, then the need to think about the subject finally started to go away, as did the anxiety. If you are spending all your day trying not to feel anxiety, then you are still giving far too much attention to it.

It is much better to acknowledge you have anxiety and decide not to let it get in the way of living your life. Don't try not to feel it. If you allow it to be there, then you have nothing to obsess and worry about. This approach will lead to your brain focusing on other subjects and you will start to feel engaged with the other things in your life and the world around you. Then one day, you will look back, and the subject will be a distant memory.

I hope that helps

So, do you see that all the research, need to fix and her obsession with the subject and how she was feeling, was creating this constant loop of thinking about herself and anxiety? Again, the way out was not to 'DO' something about it but to see what was causing it. The lady who replied had found the answer by no longer 'doing' something. She stopped feeding the subject of anxiety into her sub-conscious each day and then allowed the habit of thinking about herself and the subject to die down naturally. Also, by fully allowing herself to experience anxiety, she was allowing it to release itself. Again, she did nothing but be open to experiencing it.

Anxiety is nothing more than trapped energy within the body; energy that you have previously created through stress and worry. When anxiety rises, it is the body trying to release this energy, but because it is unpleasant to feel, so many then turn to all their rituals, techniques and distractions in an attempt to 'NOT' feel it. Due to this being the instinctive reaction to uncomfortable feelings, most believe that it is the right thing to do. But how can your body ever have a chance to release this energy that you have previously created when you won't allow its presence within you? I will repeat this often as it is so important that you grasp it. When I truly grasped this, then all attempts to fight and suppress my anxious feelings fell away. It made no sense for me to carry on doing so. In fact, I now wanted to experience this anxious energy, as I wanted to be free of it.

There is truly nothing wrong with you other than what you are creating. There is no outside force doing this to you. At your core there is nothing wrong with you, there never was. A few people can get quite defensive when I say this and respond with things like "But what about this occasion, I just felt anxious for no reason?" Yes, this is because of what you created yourself in the past through stress and worry, a lot of anxiety/negative energy is now stored up inside the body and through a process of your body trying to release it, then you may feel anxious for no real reason. But on other occasions, I can explain how they have done this to themselves and that the mind and body are working and operating exactly as they should be.

Thought is what the mind and body react and responds to. If you worry about a situation, or more likely how you feel, then, yes, of course, you are going to feel anxious. That rule is true for everyone. You may get a bigger reaction than the non-anxiety sufferer as your nerves may be a little more frayed, and you have more anxious energy stored up within you, but the same rule applies to everyone. So, it is just as important to no longer create your anxiety through more stress and worry as is it to release what you have previously created.

Many people have asked me what I did to get better and I have replied that I did not do anything other than reach a place of total surrender and non-resistance. This meant that I no longer tried to find temporary relief every time I did not feel the way I thought I should. I no longer searched around Google or tried to find a page in a book to seek any kind of comfort, and I no longer made any effort to analyse my way out of anything. I just let my mind and body go through any process it wished with as little concern as possible.

If I was flooded with negative thoughts, felt detached from my surroundings, or my anxiety was high, then I stayed in that place without making any effort to try to escape it. All I was dealing with here was past suffering; it didn't want or need me to struggle with it. If at any time you think you should not be feeling this way, that you should be calmer, happier or have more clarity, then you will be back in the cycle of fighting, struggling and suppressing.

I could feel great for days and then have a terrible day and the temptation was there to think that I should be how I was last week and just before the struggle was about to start, I would remind myself that this was all O.K. I won't try to be anywhere but where I am. That was the best single piece of advice I gave myself throughout my recovery.

'Being open' is not a technique to achieve anything, as then it can be turned into another way of controlling or suppressing feelings. It is more of an attitude than anything and one that no longer comes from a place of fear, as where there is fear there is usually resistance.

I did not always like the way I felt, and at times it could be highly challenging, but I no longer feared it. I had learnt enough to no longer be afraid of my thoughts and emotions and a lot of that came through finally allowing myself to experience them without trying to protect myself or hold distance from them. I also learnt that whatever state I found myself in, without exception it always passed.

On rare occasions, I would get caught up in trying to control and manipulate my inner state once again, as the mind is a problem-solving machine and if it does not like a particular state, then it usually seeks to escape or suppress. But once I recognised what I was doing, I would go back to a state of total allowing.

Anxious thoughts and feelings are created through excess anxious/fearful energy stored within the body. This excess energy needs to be released for you to be free of its influence; this is why allowing works. It is like the steam from a kettle. You cannot control, stop or suppress the steam coming out of the kettle as it will just keep trying to find another outlet. If it can't find this outlet, then the kettle will explode due to the steam needing to be released. In the same way, this energy that creates the anxious thoughts and feelings needs to be released. Trying to avoid or suppress this energy will just keep you in a constant state of anxious thoughts and feelings, as this energy builds up and resides within you.

I see people on my blog who help others and there are some who reach a good stage and are able to deal with things far better and pass on advice. Then there are those who have genuinely got the message. You can see it in what they write and how positive and confident they are in their words. Knowledge just flows through them. It was the same with me. I had insight after insight when I truly 'got it' and everything just started to click. I realised I had fallen for one big trick. Every single reason why I had become stuck now made complete sense. I did not have to work on one symptom through to the next; everything fell away at pretty much the same time.

Trying to fix myself was always the problem; it was never going to be the solution. I look back and think of all the effort and energy I put into trying to get better and the reason I stayed the way I did makes total sense to me now. I can't blame myself for this as I was just doing what I thought was right at that time. I will not scold anyone for what they have been doing up until now as we are all doing what we think is right. But it is like having a headache and hitting your head each day, then saying "I don't understand it. I have been hitting my head all day and I still have this damn headache! Maybe if I hit it harder tomorrow, I will get rid of it!" Yet this is what so many people do on a daily basis. It is all about getting them to recognise this and once they see it, they realise it no longer makes sense to carry on doing so.

I once helped a lady who came to me in a terrible state; she was on the verge of tears and very agitated. She explained that she had pretty much had a breakdown. She was in a very stressful and demanding job and her anxiety had gone through the roof.

She had tried numerous different approaches to get better as she needed to get back to work, her children needed her and she was worried about the effect it was having on her marriage. She also explained what had first made her feel this way. She had pushed herself so much at work and wanted a promotion so badly that she worked every hour she was asked. She was also trying to hit impossible deadlines and took her work home with her, hardly sleeping through the pressures, and all this while trying to run a family home. She said, "Paul, I feel so anxious and mentally worn out and I just don't know how to get out of it, but I have to as so many people are relying on me". I replied, "Do you see all that effort and stress you put into getting that promotion, which is the reason you felt all the stress in the first place? Well, that is exactly the worry and stress you are now putting into trying to get better". On hearing these words, a light came on and she could see what she was doing to herself. She said it was almost like looking down on herself and scolding herself for doing it.

She could not understand why it had not been obvious to her before and said, "I get it! The best way to feel better is to no longer try to feel better as this is taking me further away. Trying to feel better is actually stressing and wearing me out even more, and when it does not work, I get stressed about this also". I said, "Yes, exactly, by putting so much pressure on yourself to get better, you are creating more of what you are trying to get rid of". This lady is now back at work and taking on far less hours. She has discovered the importance of looking after herself and realises that no promotion is worth sacrificing her health.

Again, this lady was not broken, she had just moved away from her natural well-being through too much worry and stress, no one else was responsible for creating her current state but herself, no one had been responsible for her continued suffering but herself. She eventually realised that the symptoms would begin to ease if she no longer stressed and worried about the symptoms of stress and worry; this is the cycle I was able to help her to break. She did not need pills, techniques or months of counselling to get better; she just needed to see something.

None of you are broken, you have just temporarily lost yourself doing what you thought was for the best. I remember another lady saying to me, "But Paul, I am broken. Even when I allow myself to feel this way, I find little relief" I then dug deeper into this woman's story and found that she was still worrying and stressing about anything and everything outside of her anxiety.

She even said, ‘I felt a bit better, so thought it was OK to do so.”

My reply was:

“The most important thing beyond allowing yourself to feel the way you do is to no longer recreate the anxiety. Allowing yourself to feel the way you do takes all the effort, overthinking, worry and stress out of the equation and so allows a process of healing to take place, but it is just as important to no longer create it. You can’t allow and still have the mindset of worrying and stressing about life in general; otherwise, nothing will change. A real shift in your attitude and outlook on life needs to take place also. You have to realise the cause of your initial feelings too. Prevention is a far better approach than spending a lifetime looking for a cure to what you are constantly recreating”.

Chapter 2

Letting Go of Crutches

The self-help world is full of books, therapists, life coaches and all the other treatments out there, yet so many people stay stuck. Why?

I was the person with fourteen books on anxiety cures, thirty websites saved to my favourites and at the same time visiting numerous counsellors. I was continually Googling, watching online videos and wasting time and money on so-called miracle cures. It was the very early days of the Internet at that time, and if anyone said they could cure you, you believed them, but I never got anywhere and just felt worse.

Firstly, I became the subject. I fed myself the subject of anxiety day in and day out and wondered why I thought of nothing else. I became very self-aware as I was no longer interacting with the world around me and became obsessed with trying to fix myself. I was no longer Paul; I was the subject of anxiety. I woke up and carried this anxiety backpack with me wherever I went. I only threw it off to go to sleep and then it was back on first thing in the morning. Sometimes, for a split second, I would forget about the subject, but then, in an instant, it dawned on me that this was my life now. To finally get better, I thought I had to search harder, Google more, think more, look up another technique and make another appointment with a counsellor, but I could not have been more wrong.

I threw money at a lot of false promises and rubbish in my time and saw some people that I now know were not qualified to help. I did read the odd decent bit of material and did see some people who helped in some way, but years before I recovered, I remember looking at all my self-help books and thinking “I don’t need all this”. I was carrying so many statements around with me and trying to remember so much that I was constantly living inside my head. I really can’t explain what it was, but I finally knew that this was not the answer and what I really needed was a new approach.

I just had this inner knowing that if I stopped the search and left the lot unanswered, I would be OK. All that this searching seemed to do was to take me further away from my goal. Unfortunately, it was another two years before I finally let go of the self-help route because, deep down, I still believed that something was wrong with me and I was obsessed with wondering if I had missed something.

Eventually, I had just had enough. It was like some inner wisdom rose up inside me and said, “Just throw that backpack away. Throw all of your sayings, Internet favourites and safety behaviours away. You don’t need them; all this searching and struggling is just making you feel worse”. I started to look at others around me who appeared happy and carefree and I realised that these people were just going about their daily lives. They were not living in their heads trying to fix themselves. They did not have ten different sayings in order to cope with life.

My mind just felt so incredibly exhausted through all of this, yet I kept dumping more and more thinking on top of it. This was why I had lost so much consciousness and felt as though I was in a dream most of the time. I had been going over and over the subject on a daily basis and then wondered why I felt so detached from the world around me. It eventually dawned on me what I had been putting my mind and body through and how I felt had really been down to me.

The reason I had been stuck for years was because I had been looking at anxiety in the wrong way. I had spent years trying to rid myself of it and every day was just another day to try and feel better. If anxiety was around, then the battle continued. I had the idea that I must find a way to eliminate it and that if I still felt anxious, then I had failed, and so my search had to continue. Not once did I ever think to look at it in a different way and actually let the feelings be there and release them. If you ever spend your life trying not to feel something, then you will forever stay in the cycle of struggle, worry and overthinking.

Let's go back to the recognition that 'we are doing this to ourselves'.

I always thought there was something wrong with me because I felt half-baked and detached while going about my day, yet I was the one living inside my head trying to figure things out. People around me were not doing this and so all of their awareness was on the world around them. Everything to them seemed colourful and in 3D, as almost all of their focus was on their surroundings. I had 90% of my awareness on my inner world and the other 10% on the world around me, and so everything to me looked grey and flat, almost dreamlike. Yet the world was the same for all of us. The only difference was that other people were far more conscious of their surroundings because they were not stuck inside their heads, concerned about how they were feeling and worrying about how to fix themselves.

So, again, I was the one doing this to myself. If I could get out of my head and stop going over things, then I would see the world like everyone else and clarity would return. It was not something that was happening to me; it was me that was creating this flat and dull existence. I was actually walking around worrying and wondering why I felt so disconnected from the world around me when all the time it was the obsessing and worrying about being disconnected that was causing the problem. How ironic was that – constantly obsessing and searching for a solution to my disconnection ended up being the cause!

On many occasions, I would delete everything I had in my browsers, throw all my books away and just get up and live. But I only had to have one bad day and I would think that maybe I am wrong, perhaps I do need all this stuff and so I would get dragged back into my old ways. Before I knew it, I would be back in the throes of searching, worrying and fighting again. But then it hit me. I have so much suppressed anxiety, memory and habit hanging around after years of suffering, of course, I will slip back and feel anxious, lost and confused again. I just needed to be more patient and stop trying to step straight out of my suffering.

I did not need to rush for a counsellor, book or a saying the moment I felt any discomfort. If I just left myself alone, then my natural well-being would once again shine through and this is precisely what happened. I was like the person who runs around spinning plates; I was constantly running around trying to stay on top of things until one day I decided to stop and when I finally allowed the plates to fall, nothing bad actually happened.

As I write this, someone on my blog who has recovered is telling people the same thing and that he did nothing but trusted that he would always come back. Even when he felt at his lowest and was trawling through all the mind crap and anxious feelings, he resisted the need to try and fix himself. He knew that he just needed to keep trudging through the glug and truly believe and trust he would come back in time. After years of trying to stay on top of it all, he was just not going to try anymore and would open himself up to whatever arose.

This was the first time in his life that he had allowed himself to go through this process without trying to intervene. I said to him, “All you did for once in your life was to give up the battle you were having with yourself. You just let things be as they were and so no longer created so much extra suffering. This also opened the door for you to finally experience and release all these stored up negative emotions that were causing you so much pain".

We are always there ready to resurface; there is no technique needed here, no saying, no 'do'. The only 'do' is to go about your life and act in exactly the same way you would if anxiety was not around; don't change your behaviour because of how you feel. If you make a cup of tea and you feel full of dread and sadness, then carry on making that tea regardless. Don't stand there full of self-pity, trying to figure it all out, worrying and obsessing about how you feel while searching around in your mind for ways to change it. It will lift by itself if left alone; it always does. If you go on a family day out and feel like you don't want to be there, allow this feeling too. If your mind is exhausted through your past struggles, then it is entirely normal that you will feel this way, so don't curse how you feel or try to change it.

You don't have to run around trying to live life to the full to prove anything. There may be days when you need to rest and take it easy, and this is fine as long as it's not an excuse not to feel certain emotions. If you go around trying to avoid certain feelings, then inevitably you end up avoiding life. So just try to live your life as normally as you can and take these feelings with you, fully allowing for their presence as this is what eventually cures. The same applies if you are feeling detached, worn out or down. This is just a symptom of all the past introspection, worrying and overthinking you have done previously and is totally natural in the circumstances. The last thing your tired and weary mind needs now is more of the same, as this is precisely what keeps you in the cycle of feeling the way you do.

Just know that in time these emotions will pass if you are fully open to them. By doing this, you're are no longer creating more suffering by constantly trying to fix yourself and handing over your recovery to nature and your own bodies incredibly intelligent healing system. Trust me, this system works wonders when allowed to do so. The answers to eliminate suffering do not lie in anything outside of yourself.

Someone recently said to me "I have allowed, as you say, but these feelings are still there"; to which I replied: "And?" He responded by saying: "Well, I thought that if I did this, I would no longer feel anxious". I said: "You have missed the point completely and again used my words as a new technique to try and get rid of how you feel. The words were a pointer to actually allow yourself to feel how you do, not the other way around. So, yes, these feelings will still be there for a while, and they are fine to be so, as it is by allowing them to be there that will eventually free yourself of them and stop the constant rumination that keeps you in the cycle of mental exhaustion".

Let me truly clear up what I mean here so that there is no confusion. Time and time again, I see how people use my words as another way to get rid of anxiety while thinking that they are doing the opposite.

If people read what I say, thinking that by the end of the book, they will no longer have symptoms of anxiety, then they are in for a rude awakening. I am telling you the opposite. I don't want you to try and get rid of anything. I want you to give up that search for someone or something to get rid of your suffering and finally be open to experiencing it.

Allowing is not some technique to make you feel better. All it does is end the struggle, the overthinking, the resistance, the worry, suppression, focus and obsession. It puts an end to everything that was causing the majority of your suffering and finally opens the door for a process of healing to occur. When I truly understood what was needed, I realised even more the process of healing I would need to go through and that I still had past suffering to heal, and so I would have to go through a process of discomfort until I was back to my old self. Understanding alone would not release all the stored up anxious energy that I had spent years creating. It would not heal my exhausted mind instantly; it would not retrain my brain to see the world was a safe place to exist in; only time could do that.

So, I want you to let go and be open to any uncomfortable emotions you have. I want you to feel them fully and no longer try to protect yourself from them in any way. It is like opening your doors to all the unwanted visitors you have been trying to keep at bay. Your house is now open to everyone, and I mean everyone, not 'well I don't mind that, so that can come in, but I am not letting that emotion in'. It has to be a full surrender to everything, so as to give up this constant battle you are having with yourself and go through a process of releasing what has been causing you so much discomfort.

When you first open those doors, you may get a bunch of unwanted visitors; you may even feel the urge to again start kicking them out or try to distract yourself from them. But the more you stay open, the more you realise that these visitors aren't as bad as you first thought and that they aren't here to harm you. Also, the more you let them in, the less they feel like hanging around. This is the paradox, for unwanted thoughts and emotions to finally leave, they just want to be acknowledged and experienced. If you keep trying to get rid of your unwanted guests then, trust me, they will be forever knocking.

Chapter 3

Hyperawareness of oneself

A lot of people who suffer from anxiety can become very self-absorbed and preoccupied with all things personal to the exclusion of the world around them. Their interest and focus can narrow down so much on themselves and their problems that they find it incredibly difficult to be interested in anything outside of their inner world.

This constant self-focus can lead to them experiencing the feeling of being hyperaware of themselves, their thoughts and actions. They have a sense of being trapped within their own head and feel unable to truly connect to others and the world around them.

So many people have contacted me in the past and asked questions like;

So many people have contacted me in the past and asked questions like;

How can I stop thinking about myself?

How do I get out of my head?

Why do I feel so aware of myself?

How can I stop ruminating?

Why do I feel disconnected from others?

What causes these feelings of acute self-awareness?

When suffering from anxiety, many sufferers end up thinking about themselves on a daily basis. This continuous introspection occurs due to the fact that they don't feel OK inside and all the ruminating and obsessing is an attempt to fix and make sense of how they feel. Unfortunately, this constant self-focus doesn't solve their suffering. In fact, it has the opposite effect and has them feeling worse than ever.

The reason people find it difficult to stop ruminating about all things personal is that they fear letting go of the need to try and fix themselves. They feel they have to keep on top of everything and keep trying to figure a way out and if they don't, then they will lose themselves forever. Not realising that it is the very act of ruminating that is causing so many of their problems.

This obsessive ruminating is also responsible for a whole host of fresh symptoms, and so the sufferer ends up ruminating even more, which leads to a vicious cycle of trying to solve themselves. This vicious cycle occurs because the constant attempts to 'solve' end up creating the exact symptoms from which they are trying to escape from and so they just end up in a never-ending loop.

Symptoms of obsessive rumination

- Feeling trapped inside your head
- Losing connection with the outside world
- Depression
- Mental exhaustion
- Low self-esteem
- Irritability
- An overactive mind
- Trouble sleeping

Negative effects of ruminating

You don't feel part of life

When you ruminate about anything, then you narrow down your focus to that one object and so lose awareness of your surroundings. Think of your awareness as the light from a torch, if you shine the light on your inner world then you have no light/awareness for the outside world and so you no longer feel part of it.

People who are stuck in this cycle complain of being unable to properly connect to others and the world around them. This is also why a lot of sufferers tend to walk around in a dream state, a state where they struggle to take notice of their immediate surroundings. The truth is you want to feel part of your outer world; then you have to shift your awareness from your inner world back on to the external world.

It wears you out mentally

Constantly ruminating also wears you out mentally and is the primary cause of mental fatigue. The brain never gets a break and so begins to fatigue, which can cause the person to suffer from symptoms such as sleep problems, phobias, depression, irritability, lack of interest in life and a feeling of constant exhaustion.

Relationships and friendships can suffer

Continually ruminating can lead to the person unknowingly becoming very self-centred and the constant preoccupation with self can damage friendships and relationships as they have little energy or interest towards the needs of those around them and so lack that closeness and affection that all relationships need to flourish.

It can affect our mental health

Constant rumination can have a detrimental effect on our mental health and keep us stuck in a cycle of negative and unproductive thinking which can lead to feelings of depression and low self-esteem. The last place you will find mental well-being is through ruminating. Rather than helping, this constant inward focus is far more likely to maintain this distressing state of mind.

You feel trapped within your own mind and conscious of your own thoughts and actions

Continuous introspection can lead to a person feeling trapped within their own mind. This can lead them to feel hyperaware of their actions and thoughts and in a few cases, becoming hyperaware of the hyperawareness itself. This stage can be terribly frustrating as they find it hard to shift their attention from themselves to the outside world, creating a distressing feeling of enclosure.

There are many different reasons a person may be ruminating

The person with low self-esteem may constantly worry about what people think about them, continually replaying conversations they have had during the day. Their attention is not on the world around them; it is on them.

The person who suffers from social anxiety may go to a social event and spend all their night worried about how they are coming across, about what others think of them and if others are noticing how uncomfortable they are feeling. Their attention is not on the conversation; it is on them.

Someone who suffers from health anxiety may ruminate all day about some blemish, lump or bump they have found on their body while wondering if to make another appointment with the doctor. Their attention is not on the outside world; it is on them.

The person with general anxiety may spend all day at work, continually questioning why they feel like they do while mentally trying to figure a way out. Their attention is not on work; it is on them.

Others may spend all their time searching forums, googling symptoms and immersing themselves in self-help books, letting nothing else but the subject of 'fixing themselves' into their day. Their attention is not on everyday life; it is on them

They feel unless they find a solution to their problems, then they must carry on with this constant obsessing about all things personal. Many do want to give up being so self-absorbed, but it has become such a habit they don't know how.

I was the same when I suffered; it was like I could no longer get my attention off the subject of me and my inner state. I was constantly agonising over how I was feeling while mentally trying to find a way out and so lost the ability to be part of the outside world.

If I was talking to someone, my attention would always be reverting back to me, which led to me feeling incredibly enclosed and no longer part of the conversation. Even when doing everyday tasks, I found I could barely concentrate: I had a constant feeling of being trapped within my head, unable to be part of anything outside of myself, it was terribly frustrating.

Even when my anxiety symptoms had left me, I was still left with this feeling of being overly aware of myself and found it hard to find joy in anything as I never felt fully part of it. I initially fought this feeling of enclosure and tried to overcome it through more deep thinking and fighting. When this did not work, I then tried to ignore it or force my attention outside of myself and when these practices also failed, I was at a loss of what to do and thought I was stuck this way forever.

After much reflection, I finally came to the conclusion that all my desperate attempts to try and defeat this symptom had me back to thinking about myself and so my awareness was on me more than ever. It also became obvious that the very act of trying to ignore it was also another way of thinking about it. Much like the 'Try not to think of a pink elephant' and so all you do is think about pink elephants.

I now understood that my awareness was continuously focused on me through nothing more than a habit that I had created. All I had thought about for years was me and my inner state, and so, of course, my awareness was now focused there. I had a profound realisation that it wasn't me that was thinking about myself; it was the habit I had created in my brain that was. This was the very reason I could not defeat it or instantly stop thinking about myself, as this habit was overriding all my attempts to do so.

So, the way out was to finally give up obsessing about me and this feeling of enclosure, to stop trying to constantly solve myself and just go back to living. While doing so, I also had to understand that the habit to think about me and my inner world would most likely go on for a while, but I would accept this as part of my old habit and no longer try to escape or fix it.

Freedom eventually came through me, allowing myself to experience this feeling of hyperawareness without adding any resulting anxiety around it. It was my fear of it that was the problem, my fear of the feeling itself, the fear I would be stuck this way forever and would never be able to enjoy life again.

The more I feared it, the more my brain obsessed about it and tried to solve it. I finally realised that this was never about trying to fix it or distract myself from it; it was about becoming more accepting of it. Trying to solve it or distract myself from it again came from a place of fear and just kept it at the forefront of my mind. Also, all my past attempts at solving it just had me retreating back into myself, which obviously made things worse because the loop happened precisely because I was overly turned inward.

Learning to put my attention back on the world around me

At first, it took a huge leap of faith to no longer obsess about all things personal, as this had been a habit for so long. When I gave up, there was a huge pull to go back to doing so. This is what the brain does with a habit; it tries to drag you back into the familiar, just like the smoker who has a huge pull to put a cigarette back in their mouth.

My habit was to fall back into trying to fix myself, and it took some willpower to override this pull. I just knew I had to change and so just gave up all the obsessing and attempts to solve myself and went back to living my life while accepting myself as I was, especially this constant feeling of self-awareness.

Learning to finally let go

I called this stage 'my ultimate drop' where I just surrendered and gave up trying to change anything. I would just completely allow everything to be as it is. I concluded that if I did this, then the mind would have nothing left to obsess about, control or attempt to fix.

As I said previously, the obsessing and ruminating was due to me not feeling OK inside and so the way out had to come through me now being fine with not feeling OK, even if I felt an irritable, anxious mess. I could never get out of this state through ruminating more, as it was the very ruminating that was responsible for me feeling so self-aware and having little to no connection to others and the world around me

I knew on a very deep level that if I wanted to be part of the world around me, then I had to take my focus off my inner world and put it back on the outer world. I actually had a huge insight into this very fact when I was attempting to communicate with my mother while she was writing an email. As she so was engrossed in the email, all I got back from the conversation was the odd mumble. It was evident that she couldn't talk to me while her attention was on what she was doing.

I then realised that this is why I didn't feel part of life and why I felt so half-baked and detached from my surroundings, as none of my attention was out there, it was all on me. My mother wasn't part of the conversation because her awareness was barely on it, she couldn't put it on two things at once, just as I could not put it on my inner state and my surroundings. This is the only reason I felt so detached and not because something was deeply wrong with me.

I now realised why I struggled so much to be part of a conversation, as it was very difficult to be interested and part of a conversation when all my attention was focused inwards. I finally saw that there was nothing wrong with me and again I was responsible for the way I felt, and it was me and only me who could get my way out of it this cycle I found myself in.

I knew this wasn't going to happen overnight and I would have to stay committed to it. So, the first thing I had to do was to stop obsessing about me, my inner state and this very feeling of hyperawareness. I had to accept that I had created this habit and it was going to run for a while, but I was no longer going to put any more fuel into it by trying to fix or escape it.

I could not get frustrated with this past habit; I could not defeat it. I just had to go back out there, begin to live and engage with the world around me and allow my focus to naturally shift towards other things. At first, it was difficult to feel part of my surroundings as I continued to feel very self-aware, but I had to allow this feeling to be present with utter acceptance and carry on regardless. With this new understanding and approach, the habit of thinking about myself started to fall away and my awareness slowly but surely shifted back to my surroundings.

With this shift in awareness, everything seemed much more colourful, almost in 3D and I began to notice and appreciate things I had not seen before. I started to see the beauty around me instead of being constantly obsessed with myself.

I had finally understood what was causing this problem and cut out the root of it rather than continue working on the symptoms and was able to shift my focus back to where it always should have been.

To finish, here is a reply from a contributor to my blog to someone who asked how he got over the habit of thinking about himself.

Without trying to, trying not to think about yourself is just another way of thinking about yourself. I just basically said: 'OK I guess this is what I will be thinking about for a while now" and it eventually went away.

Chapter 4

The Anxiety Loop

Here I am going to explain the anxiety loop in which so many people find themselves in and how people misinterpret the whole route to recovery. You will have read a lot of what I say here in different parts of the book, but I think it is very important for people to fully understand this loop so they can finally be free of it. This understanding is so crucial to recovery.

No one told me this and I did not read it anywhere; it just came to me one day when I was putting the pieces of the puzzle together. When this realisation came, I just saw it so clearly. Any questions or doubts I had about whether or not I was on the right track disappeared and I made a huge leap towards recovery.

Firstly, anxiety is energy that is initially created in the body through the power of thought. You cannot feel stressed or worried without first having a worrisome thought; this is how our bodies work. And it is this worrisome thought that creates the energy in the body that creates the feeling of being anxious. Now the odd concern or worrisome thought is fine, as when the worry or concern is over then the energy is released as it has no fuel to build-up and so we go back to a place of calm. The only way people reach a state of constant anxiety is when they stress or worry over a prolonged period of time and so this energy is continually created and not released, or there is more created than has a chance to be released. Due to this, it then begins to be stored within the body, and so you feel this anxious energy constantly. You have now reached the stage of being continually anxious.

When people get to this stage, they don't understand why. They also have no intention of feeling this anxiety and so they go on a mission to find the answer to eliminate it. They search everywhere for the answer on how to do this, hitting one brick wall after another, and this is where they can enter the next stage.

The next stage of the loop is when they start to worry about their anxiety and try to fight it off or suppress it. But any attempt to suppress, deny or change an emotion takes immense energy. This constant expenditure of energy is what drains you and leaves you feeling so worn out and weary. Also, all this constant worry and struggle actually creates is more anxious energy and so it just keeps building up within. So unbeknown to the sufferer, every attempt to eliminate or control their anxiety just creates more of the very thing from which they are trying to escape.

The next stage comes because they either dislike or in most cases, fear these emotions and so they begin to hide away and go down the path of avoidance, hoping that one day it will go away. Avoidance is yet another technique to deny emotions, so they again stay trapped inside the body as they have nowhere else to go. Not only that, but due to this avoidance, the sufferer is falsely teaching their mind that the outside world is something to fear. This can then lead to their mind producing the fear response in non-threatening situations. So, trying to avoid or run away from emotions can never solve the problem; all it does is begin to restrict your life.

The only way people can truly recover is to give up the worry and stress that creates all this anxious energy in the body and then allow a release to happen. This means no more fighting, no more suppressing and no more worrying, as you cannot empty a cup that you keep on refilling. If you want to rid yourself of this energy, the answer is to feel it without adding any more to it; this is the only way. This is why people sometimes search around for years, yet never find the answer to how to get rid of anxiety, as the answer is not to try to get rid of it, but to allow a release of it.

Even now, people misinterpret what I say when I tell them to allow the anxiety to manifest itself. They think this is some kind of technique to not feel it. It is not; it is pointing them in the completely opposite direction, which is to not only be fully open to its presence but to welcome it, as allowing a release will eventually empty all that stored up anxious energy within them.

However, the crucial mistake a lot of people make, is they think that if they are still feeling it, then they must be doing something wrong, so they then go back to searching, avoiding, fighting, worrying, fixing and suppressing.

If you are always worried about your current state or are anxious about being anxious, the anxiety just ends up being recreated and so the cycle continues. This is the very reason people stay stuck for years because they stay in the never-ending loop of trying not to feel this anxious energy.

As you can now see, I did not eliminate anxiety; I just allowed a process of release to happen without adding more to it. This is why I no longer feel anxious unless there is a reason. Any anxiety I feel would need to be activated by an anxious thought in a real situation. But your anxiety doesn't need a thought to be activated as it is stored up in your body and can be felt at any time for no reason; this is what throws people. They think 'It's still there so I must keep searching'.

So, this is the cycle; the more you try to eliminate anxiety, the more of it you create. When you truly understand this loop, then you no longer try to suppress this energy, as you know this will just keep it stored up within the body. You no longer battle to rid yourself of it because you realise this will just wear you out mentally and you no longer worry about it (creating more anxiety) as you now understand its presence and the process you have to go through, so the whole anxiety loop is broken.

When this release is allowed to happen without you creating more, the anxiety will start to subside. It will become weaker and will arrive less often as your stores are beginning to empty. When the stores are entirely empty, then you no longer feel anxious at inappropriate times and you go back to your natural default setting.

This is why setbacks aren't really setbacks at all but just another release. It is the not worrying about or trying to manipulate this release of energy that eventually cures.

The same loop applies to anxious thinking

When we are anxious this stored up energy does not just release itself through emotions, it also releases itself through the mind as well as the body and this is why the person can also suffer from intrusive, anxious or fearful thoughts. It is just all this accumulated energy releasing itself. You may notice that if you feel fearful, anxious or unsettled, this is when you experience more of this kind of thinking and the calmer you feel, the less you do, which of course supports what I am saying.

So, if this release of anxious/negative energy manifests itself through thoughts, then you again have to allow this release to happen, as any attempt to fight, worry and suppress what is coming up just creates more anxious energy and more irrational thoughts. Do not be thrown by whatever thoughts come up as this energy can manifest itself in many ways; an intrusive thought is just anxious/fearful energy, releasing itself through the mind. There is no reason to take these thoughts seriously, as they hold no truth and have no bearing on reality.

So, if your thoughts race, then allow them to race; if they become obsessive, then let them be obsessive; if they appear scary then allow them to be scary. I used to have some real thought storms and once I saw them as just energy storms, all the fear went out of them. I could now see them as simply a release of energy and nothing to be concerned about. With this new insight I was able to just let this energy pass on through me without concern and the more I released this energy through a process of allowing, the more the intrusive thoughts began to weaken.

The main reason my thoughts no longer race and are no longer scary or obsessive is because all this negative/anxious energy is no longer stored up within me. Can you now see how pointless and counter-productive all this battle and concern about your thoughts is? Remember, recovery is never about trying to eliminate anything; this just creates the opposite effect. It is all about seeing something.

So, there is your loop, hopefully, now people realise that you cannot reach peace without feeling some discomfort along the way, as it is all a very important part of the recovery process. So, the next time you feel anxious or unsettled, don't spend your day pointlessly trying to get out of it, see it as your mind and body finding its own way back to peace through a process of releasing old energies.

Chapter 5

What is the need for Fear and Anxiety?

When we reach the stage of feeling constantly anxious, it is our body and mind's way of telling us that we have overdone things and that we are overworking our system. It is telling us to slow down and take it easy. It is an inbuilt warning system just doing its job, but again it does not come with instructions, so many people don't get this message and instead of taking it easy they end up putting more of a burden upon themselves. The mind and body are then thinking 'Huh? What are you doing? I need a break. That's what I am trying to tell you. The last thing I need is more effort, worry and overthinking'.

It is also helpful to know that so much of anxiety comes from thought. When someone says, "It's the money problems I have that have made me anxious", it is not. It is your thoughts about your money problems that made you anxious. You can swap this for 'The problems at work or in my marriage', but it is never the circumstances, or shall we say life situations, which bring on anxiety, it is our thoughts about our life situation. I would encourage people not to say 'I have anxiety', but instead say, 'I have unknowingly created anxiety'.

An example would be: two people are due to visit the dentist to have exactly the same work done. One worries himself into a total state while the other does not worry at all. They both face the same situation but have two completely different experiences. It is never the situation, just your thoughts about the situation, which causes the anxiety. It is very helpful to know this so we can get a sense of the fact that we are the sole creators of our anxiety and therefore have the power to no longer create it.

Don't fear, fear

The fear response is also a built-in system in all of us. It is there to warn us of danger. It is there for a reason and that reason is to protect us. It was never meant to work against us. My own understanding of the fact that it was built in to protect me made me realise that it would never harm me in any way. Who or what you believe created us would never be that cruel.

The fear response is nothing more than a harmless protection system that is necessary for us to survive. Yes, it's not a particularly comfortable system, but if it didn't create these uncomfortable feelings, we would not run away from that man who was standing in front of us with a knife or try to escape from that snarling dog. The feeling of fear is supposed to feel scary so as to prepare us for action or escape.

I eventually stopped trying to suppress my own fear reaction when I realised it was part of being human. I saw it as just another energy I was capable of experiencing. Through understanding, I just began to be far more comfortable with it. Actually, just seeing my fear as energy helped me to view it in a completely different light. Although it still felt uncomfortable, a lot of my fear of it went away, due to this, I was more open to its presence and it no longer had any real influence on my life.

A lady once said to me "It's not fair, I can't go to the supermarket because I feel such fear. I am OK going to my local shop, but not the supermarket" I said: "The supermarket is no more threatening than the corner shop. What could be scary about a row of baked beans? Nothing! What you really fear is the way you will feel when you get there. The reason you don't feel that way when visiting your corner shop is that you don't have the same thoughts about it, your perception is different and so your mind does not trigger the same fear response.

If I go to the supermarket, I do not have one fearful thought about it and hence I do not feel any fear. So, the danger is not in the supermarket; it never was. The supermarket is in no way a scary place in which to be and it is only your past memories and thoughts about it that make it seem so. If you are open to feeling this fear response wherever you are, then you can go anywhere you wish. When you allow yourself to feel the emotion of fear, then you are not only allowing a release of this energy, but you are also guiding your mind to turn this fear response down. This is because it understands through your continued actions that you are safe; on the other hand, if you keep avoiding, then you are sending it the opposite message.

Non-sufferers who feel fear at appropriate times hardly bother when they do so. Some, such as adrenalin junkies, actually like it. It is those that feel it when they deem it to be happening at inappropriate times that fear the feeling and in a lot of cases associate it to the situation they are in, as though it is a genuine threat.

If you fear the actual feeling of fear, then it makes sense that the feeling will be much stronger, as what you are doing is adding another layer of worry on top of the initial feelings. Your mind senses you are scared of something, so it shoots in some extra adrenalin to give you the option to escape. Again, your system is working fine and just following the information it is receiving from you.

I will give you a personal example. I used to play indoor football once a week. There were quite a few people there and when I was at my worst, it was quite daunting for me. I was OK when I was lost in the game, but with so many people about, some of whom I may have to engage with, getting changed beforehand filled me with fear. I remember getting changed at home on some occasions so that I would not have to go into the changing rooms, and if I did have to go in, I would get changed as quickly as possible.

For a few hours, before I went, I would be going over it in my mind and making sure I got changed near the door. Looking back on that now, who was creating this fear? ME! Who was teaching my mind that the whole experience was a threat? ME! That changing room was the same for everyone. It was no different for me than it was for all the others, and no one else was looking to get changed at home or worrying hours beforehand, rushing to get ready. I was the one that created this danger that never actually existed. My mind or, as I will regularly call it throughout this book, my computer was doing everything it should. I was telling it there was danger here, so my fear response was on high alert for non-existent threats, ones that I had created.

One person was worrying, and nine others were not. Who was the one that felt fearful? Was this a coincidence? All these fearful/worrisome thoughts and actions had nothing to do with the situation I was in; they were all built around the fear of feeling fear. The answer for me was to understand fear better and so lessen my fear of it, not spend my whole life trying not to feel it as I had previously done.

Once I got this insight, I saw numerous other occasions where I was doing it to myself. The approaching neighbour that I saw coming down the street and my thoughts would be 'Oh no, please don't see me' and when she did, I would have more thoughts about how to get away quickly. When I felt the inevitable fear, I would then blame it on the neighbour or rack myself with self-pity about my own plight thinking some outside force was doing this to me. But I had created every bit of it through my thinking and my actions; the computer was just following what I was feeding it and was working fine. There was nothing wrong with the system and there was nothing wrong with me. I was doing this to myself and I was beginning to see this now.

So, what did I do and how did things change?

The realisation that there was not a single thing in my daily life to be genuinely anxious about and that this was all coming through my thoughts about situations and not the situations themselves was a massive insight for me. If there was truly nothing to be anxious about and other people managed fine, then these fears really did not exist. They were all self-created through my faulty perceptions and desire to not feel uncomfortable; it could not be anything else.

So, I was not going to be tricked anymore by my anxious thinking and I started to no longer follow it blindly, but to actually catch it. All those weeks of worrying about the indoor football and all the other places I had added to my list had been stored in my computer. It had registered that there was danger before, so when it saw the football court, the old doubts would surface and the computer would send through some adrenalin and the old automatic thoughts of 'go for the bench by the door' would appear. But I recognised that a lot of these thoughts were now conditioned, like an automatic response, but they were still only thoughts. It was up to me whether or not I identified with them and followed them via my behaviour.

I realised that my brain was just going into its memory bank and trying to keep me safe, so I just thanked it for trying to keep me safe but told it I was fine and I didn't need its help or protection anymore. Previously, I had followed my thoughts blindly and never brought awareness to them. I believed them without actually seeing them for what they were – an old conditioned response - and I never questioned them. I realised that I was just stuck in old, conditioned thinking; an old belief system that was not who I was and that had no truth in it whatsoever.

I eventually got so good at catching my faulty thinking that it became automatic and so I no longer followed my previous instinct to avoid or escape. Another example was when I was out walking with my friend and we walked past an old school friend's house. My friend said, "Come on, let's go and say hello and have a coffee with him". All these thoughts of 'make an excuse; what will I say; he will notice how uncomfortable I am; no, I can't', flooded through me and so I took a step back and truly saw them as just old conditioned thoughts and not actual reality and so made a decision to bypass them.

So, I said, "Sure let's go and say hello" and the difference was amazing. I was still a little anxious but fine. Before, I would have either made an excuse not to go in, thinking I had made another lucky escape or gone into the situation and had a constant running commentary about how awful this was, wondering how I was coming across and what to say next, and it would have been a bit of a disaster.

From that day on, if any insecure or past conditioned thoughts did come up, I just saw them for what they were, serving me no purpose and I just let them go without following them. The old conditioned thoughts were never the problem; the problem only occurred if I identified with them, took them to be true and adjusted my behaviour accordingly. I started to see my mind as just a conditioned machine and the fears it created were merely due to my past behaviour and did not exist in reality. That one incident and insight had such a positive bearing on my future.

A few days later my neighbour was washing his car and instead oy my usual shouting hello and getting in my car before he could start talking, I went right over there and started a conversation. Once again, when I saw right through the thoughts about it being something to fear and run away from it went so much better. I was now sending back a completely different message and my body/mind responded differently. It did not go perfectly by any means, but far better than ever before. I finally realised that I did not have to be a slave to my old conditioned thinking and I could deal with a few uncomfortable feelings. In fact, now I had brought some awareness to my thinking, I could start to smile at it and a lot of it now seemed silly and certainly not worth following. Also, the less belief I put into it, the more it began to fade.

What I was going against and changing here were old neural pathways in my brain that had been created through my past beliefs, actions and conditioning. Your subconscious mind is nothing more than a collection of limiting beliefs, negative conditioning and misguided perceptions about life that you have taken to be true.

The reason we need and rely on our subconscious mind in life is so that we don't have to relearn how to drive a car or tie our shoelaces each day and why it helps when it becomes an automatic behaviour. So, as you can see, we need it for our existence. It is only when we create a behaviour that hinders our life or take on a faulty belief to be true that a problem occurs.

A belief could be someone being continually told they are ugly and worthless by another person and so they eventually believe this to be true. They have taken on this false belief to be fact and so it enters their subconscious and, no matter what anyone else says to the contrary, nothing can shift them from this image they now have of themselves. This was true of my own struggle with social anxiety. The belief that I wasn't interesting and no one would want to talk to me eventually became subconscious. It was a complete belief on my part, and so I would avoid social interaction or fall into people-pleasing behaviours. It wasn't until I was able to see through these faulty subconscious beliefs and no longer support them, that they started to slowly fall away and my social anxiety left me.

The problem is these pathways are not always easy to break down, as due to the mind wanting you to stay in your current conditioning, they create a big pull and some discomfort within you if you try to go against them. This is why some people can understand on an intellectual level but then get dragged back into their past behaviour as the pathway has yet to be reprogrammed into a new one. The intellectual mind is saying one thing and the subconscious mind is saying another, and so, at first, it isn't easy as there is an inner war going on and hence you feel the pull to go back to your old behaviours, even after you understand what is happening.

It is just like a smoker who gives up cigarettes but still finds a tremendous pull within them to light up another. They actually don't want another cigarette but are just feeling the pull of the addiction. If they can ride this out without giving in to it, then the pull/addiction will fall away and the need to light up again will no longer be there.

You just have to understand what is going on and learn to ignore this initial pull to follow old behaviours that are not serving you. To keep living the life you want and then, in time, you begin to build a new pathway. This is exactly how I got past all my old irrational fears and began to live the life I wanted. I realised that knowledge alone was never going to break down these old pathways; only action would.

So, there is no point reading books and hoping that tomorrow everything will be behind you. You have to go out and practice going against your old conditioned responses, seeing them for what they are and no longer supporting them by following them blindly or showering them with belief. You can always bypass any past response, be it a thought or an emotion and live the life you wish, no matter what the pull to follow them is.

Just remember that these pathways can take a while to change. It may be a few weeks, maybe months, depending on your commitment to changing them. But I guarantee that if you keep living the life you want and stop following these old pathways, then new ones will be built and your old behaviours and reactions will change. This does take a leap of faith and some courage, but once I understood this process, I actually enjoyed it. I liked putting myself out there and seeing all these old belief systems and behaviours break down and change into new positive ones.

My favourite quote by Van Gough sums this up perfectly;

"If you hear a voice within you say 'you cannot paint' then by all means paint and that voice will be silenced."

This is exactly what happened to me. If ever that voice told me I shouldn't do something, then I did it, and eventually, the voice of old conditioned thinking became silent.

So, start to catch your thoughts and question them. "Is there really any danger here, or am I just taking my old conditioned thinking seriously and supporting a false belief?" Start to bring some awareness to your conditioned thinking/patterns instead of following them blindly.

Remember:

'Unless there is an obvious danger in front of you then there is not a single thing in the outside world to get anxious about. Only your thoughts about situations can hold you back. It is seeing the lie behind these thoughts that creates a shift in your perception'.

Chapter 6

Struggling with your Thoughts

Before I begin this chapter, it is vital for you to understand that an anxious person with a mind full of negative/fearful energy may find that their thoughts are more obsessive and fear-based than most. When your anxiety levels drop, and your mind is less active, then your thoughts begin to change automatically. It is not your job to try and change them and nor do you need to; it is just for you to see them for what they are – thoughts that are brought on by your current state and so have no bearing on reality.

When you are dealing with anxiety, these thoughts mainly arise because there is a lot of negative/anxious energy stored up within you and this energy can then manifest itself into unpleasant and, in some cases, obsessive thoughts. I have known people instantly understand this simple fact and never take another anxious/intrusive thought seriously again. With this new understanding, they realise these thoughts no longer have any real substance and so they ultimately lose their fear of them. Without this fear, then these thoughts no longer have their attention or respect and are just seen as a flow of negative/anxious energy being released through the simple power of thought.

If one thing comes up more than anything else on my blog and Facebook pages, it is the subject of people's thinking, be it 'I can't stop thinking; my thoughts are obsessive and horrible; my inner voice is so critical' and many more.

I know this will probably be the chapter most people want to read and it is one I am keen to write in order to stop people needlessly suffering this way. I did cover it in my original book, but not only did I want to give people more of an understanding, but also a way of genuinely helping with this inner commentary. The reason people get so stuck here is that once again they do the complete opposite of what they should.

The reality is that we all think. Thoughts help guide us through life and they are an essential part of your physiological makeup that gives flavour to our experience. You can meditate for hours, climb up a mountain in Tibet or sit under a tree in Timbuktu, but you will always think. There is absolutely nothing wrong with thinking; without it, we could not operate.

Stopping thinking

A lot of people say to me "I can't stop thinking" and I always say, "Neither can I and nor can anyone else, so don't try". The very act of trying not to think just adds more thinking on top. Another thing that is impossible to do is to try to change the content of your thinking through personal will. No one knows what they are going to think in the next five minutes, so it is a completely pointless exercise to try and change your thoughts or attempt to suppress them. The way out of negative thinking is not achieved through force or suppression, the way out is to no longer identify with it.

This is why affirmations rarely work as the very act of trying to use an affirmation is a clear sign that you have put belief into a negative thought. For example, if you get a negative thought that says 'My life is awful and I will never feel happy', reading an affirmation that says 'Your life is what you make it, keep on the right path and happiness will arrive at your door' may make you feel hopeful for a few minutes, but it won't be long before those old critical thoughts pop back up and pull you down. Also, the fact that you have been thinking this way for months and in a lot of cases years will ensure that your old conditioned thoughts have the last word and shout the loudest, and within a short period of time the affirmation's effect will be gone, and the old critical thinking will be back.

If you want to be free of negative thinking, then you have to deny it any fuel and its fuel is your belief and interest in it. This is why it makes me smile when I see these books saying 'How to change your thinking and be happy' - well, good luck there. A far better and more suitable title for a book would be:

'No longer take your thinking seriously!'

I remember once reading a book and the author said: "I went to Thailand and the mountains of Tibet trying to silence my mind, when the answer all along was to no longer identify with my negative thoughts".

How true; the real freedom is in being able to think anything and no longer care and then the battle with your thoughts is over. There really is then no need to change or struggle with any thought that arises, if you no longer identify with it as the truth, then it holds no power and no longer appears as reality.

Any attempt to stop your thoughts is fruitless and counter-productive, as the very effort to prevent a thought is a thought in itself and how can you stop a thought with another thought? It just ends up in another loop of the mind trying to silence itself through more thinking.

So, if we can't forcefully stop or change our thoughts, then what do we do?

Well, firstly, we need to create a different relationship with them. If you no longer take your thinking seriously, then nothing is off-limits. So, nothing needs to be done, and nothing needs to be changed, which means you can think anything you wish. How liberating is that? If you are forever holding on to the so-called good thoughts and trying not to think the negative ones, then you are in for one internal battle that will mentally drain you.

Trying to rid yourself of unwanted thoughts is like playing the game 'whack-a-mole'. Once you try and suppress one, then another one will pop up and take its place. This is something I once did on a daily basis. It was truly exhausting and went absolutely nowhere towards solving the problem.

After the penny finally dropped my mind created the same negative/intrusive thoughts for quite a while, but the thing that changed was my attitude towards them. I will say this more than once as it is very important: **Identification with your thoughts is what causes the suffering, not the thoughts themselves**. It is a bit like seeing a person in a gorilla suit. At first, it may scare you as you perceive it to be a real gorilla, but once you know it's just a person in a suit, it no longer bothers or concerns you. Thoughts are like that. At first, they may appear real and scary and worthy of your attention, but when you see them for what they truly are, then you no longer fear them or take them seriously and the ongoing battle to change or suppress them ceases. They just become internal noise that no longer bothers you or hold your attention.

Through developing a far better understanding of how the mind operates, I no longer resisted or feared my thoughts. In fact, when a lot of them popped up, I would smile at them and think "Wow, I remember how I used to take that one seriously." There were no good or bad thoughts anymore and I did not label them as such. They were all the same to me now, just thoughts passing through my consciousness. At one time I took them seriously, grabbed hold of them, chewed on them and when this did not pacify me, I attempted to ignore them or push them away. Basically, they had my full respect and threw me around like a washing machine.

People say to me "Yes, but when I think something bad then I have an awful feeling afterwards. This is why I try to stop or control my thoughts. It's OK for you to say, 'just let them pass right on through', but they really bother and affect me". I reply by saying, "The thought is not the problem and the thought is not the reason you have an emotional reaction. The reason you have a huge reaction is because of your fear and resistance to that thought. It is your complete identification with it that brings on the emotional reaction, not the thought itself. At first, my own thoughts did not change, but my identification and fear towards them did, and that is why there was no longer an accompanying reaction and why they no longer controlled my behaviour.

So, if the content of my thinking did not change, then it is obvious that my attitude towards them did, as what other explanation could there be for them no longer bothering or influencing me? Even if there still is an accompanying reaction through habit, then allow that reaction to come without more fear and resistance and just take the hit. You will soon lose interest in this too".

It is never the thought that is the problem, and it never was. It is the fear and belief in it that brings on the emotional reaction. I understand thoughts now and realise that they are just forms of energy passing through with no substance. Because of this, no thought can touch me now the way it used to and I, like most people, still have some fearful or insecure thoughts from time to time. But that's all they are to me now, just a thought. I now live my life and accept whatever thoughts pass through.

So, to recap, it is resistance and identification with your thinking that causes suffering. For years I falsely believed that it was the other way around, that it was my thinking that was causing the problem and this is what needed changing. I tried affirmations, therapists, numerous techniques and all to no avail as I was looking in completely the wrong direction. I did not need to change my thinking, nor did I need to try and silence it. These very acts had created a monster, as in attempting to stop or change my thinking, it had gone up tenfold. I was trying to get out of my own head and had only succeeded in getting stuck in it further. I had entered a cycle of thinking about thinking, trying to stop thinking with more thinking and if I had stuck to this path, I would still be doing it to this day.

Your personal thoughts are not reality; they are just your own perception of reality.

I once helped a lady overcome her health anxiety by telling her about my social anxiety days and how taking my thinking seriously was the major factor in me continuing to struggle.

She said “Oh no, I am fine socially, that doesn't bother me at all” I replied: “The only difference between you and me is that my thinking was different from yours. You had no thoughts about being unworthy like I did, and I had no thoughts about a spot on my nose being cancer”. I explained to her that it was her belief in her thinking that had her ringing the doctor twenty times a week and mine had me people pleasing and avoiding interactions. If we had swapped thoughts, then I would have been ringing the doctor and she would have been avoiding interactions. When I explained it to her this way, it hit her really hard. She said, “Paul, I get what you are saying; these thoughts aren't true, are they? That was a brilliant way of explaining it and I now understand what you mean. It is not the thought of a harmless spot on my nose being cancer that has me ringing the doctor; it is my belief in this thought that does!”

She finally got it! It is the belief in our thinking that causes the problem, not the thoughts themselves, and so that is where the answer lies. Running to her doctor every other day was not going to solve her problems. She would only find freedom when she learnt to no longer identify with her thoughts and not give in to the pull of following them. It was the same with my social anxiety. While I continued to put belief into these thoughts, then nothing was ever going to change.

The woman mentioned above suffered from health anxiety after a visit to the doctor, where he missed something that was picked up by someone else. Due to her anxious state at the time, her mind went into overdrive about him missing something again. She then latched on to this fearful thinking, put loads of belief into it and so the thought about them 'missing something' grew and so it kept repeating in her mind. She would then see a minor blemish or feel a minor discomfort and believe she was seriously ill, and so keep making appointments to see the doctor. No matter how many times the doctor and any other specialist told her that she was fine, the anxious thought that there was something wrong, spoke much louder, and so she was forever going back for a second opinion.

If it wasn't for her anxious state the first time he had missed something, then she would have just realised that the doctor made a one-off, rare mistake and so that thought would not have manifested itself. What she should have done is to see that the thought was created due to her current anxious state and just let it go. It was only due to her putting loads of interest and belief into this thought that it grew and became a subconscious belief that no one could pacify.

It took some awareness and understanding for her to eventually see through the thought and how it was created. It was only through doing this that she was finally able to no longer put belief into it and hence the need to ring her doctor every other day finally ceased.

As you can see, the term 'health anxiety' is just a label given out to nothing more than putting belief into a thought and then giving in to the pull of following it. So many needless labels are given out to people. These labels have them believing there is something inherently wrong with them, not realising they have a logical explanation and can be easily overcome through a simple understanding.

Another woman once contacted me, explaining how her thoughts were ruining her life. She said that the anxiety had started after her mother died and then the thoughts had followed. She stated that she would get very paranoid about the people around her, thinking that everyone disliked her. She also had a lot of self-critical thoughts about not being good enough and that her husband could do far better.

After a brief chat where I explained how anxiety could create a lot of this type of thinking, I asked her if she had always thought this way. She said: "No, only in the last year since my mother died and the anxiety arrived". I said: "Well, if you did not think them last year, then these thoughts can't be true. She replied: "Yes, I understand that, but they have such an effect on me and make me feel awful, unwanted and disliked - that emotion is real". I said: "They only have such an effect on you because you perceive them to be true. At the moment, you are totally identifying with them. You don't see them as untrue like you say, because if you did you would not get any reaction to them.

It is because you believe the thoughts that everyone hates you and that your husband could do better that you have an emotional reaction to them and why they feel real and solid. You are not seeing them as just a by-product of your current anxious state and overall mood; one which is only increasing due to your belief in these thoughts.

I also said: "I am not here to help change your thoughts. They will do that by themselves once your anxiety lessens and you stop showering them with belief. That is all you need to do - see them for what they are and no longer put belief into them.

In doing this then they will lose their punch and have little or no effect on you". I helped this lady for a while after this initial conversation and eventually, she saw the truth behind her thinking and sent me this message.

Hi Paul,

Thanks to your wonderful advice I am doing so much better and the negative thoughts have all but gone now. If a negative/self-critical thought does come up, I just give it full permission to be there. I just allow the thought dance about until it realises it is not getting any respect from me and it then fizzles out. I know now that, in the past, it was me identifying with thoughts and seeing them as real that caused my emotional reaction and created more anxiety within me, which in turn only led to more anxious thinking, brought my mood down further and kept me in the cycle.

Not only that, but because I believed them, it was also affecting my behaviour. Because I believed the thought that people no longer liked me, I would then try and please everyone and because I believed the thought that my husband could do better, I would start arguments with him just to check that he did still love me. He told me afterwards that he was baffled as to why I suddenly thought this would not be true and then I felt pretty damn awful for starting the arguments (another reason to no longer believe my anxious thinking). I look back now and realise I did not feel this way because of any thought, but because I believed my anxious thoughts. Yet these thoughts really had no substance, only my belief in them made them appear real. This lesson will also help me beyond my anxiety, so thank you so much for all your help and advice.

Thoughts aren't reality

People think that because they think something then, of course, it must be true. How many times have you seen someone take offence at something that does not make sense to you? This was because they had a thought about a particular situation that seemed real to them. It was not fact, but they believed it to be and bought into it. I know someone who is very sensitive to the point where you have to really watch what you say to him. People regularly say that he always gets the wrong end of the stick and blows up, and he has lost a lot of friends through it. I once blamed him, but now I realise that he is not a bad person; he is just taking his false thinking about certain situations seriously. If he could learn to no longer do this, he would not have the reactions he does, and that would lead to a much easier life for him with far less confrontation.

Below is a genuine encounter I once had which illustrates the fact that thoughts are not reality and that we don't have to believe them.

I had a friend who was seeing a woman who had been cheated on, beaten and verbally abused by an ex-partner. I was also friends with the girl and we often went out for a meal as a foursome. The friend would often tell me he was going to break up with her as he could never do anything right. She constantly phoned him when he was out, accused him of things he had not done and was continually looking for his reassurance that he would not leave her. He said he loved her very much, but that he could not go on like this. I asked if he would let me talk to her, to which he agreed.

On speaking to her, she said she really loved him, but these thoughts of him leaving her kept coming up. She was also waiting for the first punch to come and she couldn't understand why he was nice to her. Surely, he had a hidden agenda. When he went out, she was also scared he would meet someone else. I looked at her and could see nothing but dysfunctional thinking that had nothing to do with reality. Her past had just conditioned her to think this way. He was not going to cheat, hit or leave her. These thoughts were there, yes, but they were completely false. However, she had bought into the fact that because she thought them, they must be real. She could have had a fantastic relationship in the past, met him and her thoughts about this relationship would have been entirely different. I told her that the only way to save this great relationship was to no longer take these thoughts seriously. Allow them to come up if they wanted to, but realise that they are just a product of past experiences and old conditioned thinking that held no truth whatsoever. Thinking this way was not the problem and these thoughts could never affect her or her relationship, only believing them could. I finished by saying to her "Please don't let the content of your thinking due to past experiences ruin your future".

What she had done in the past was push partners away because she believed her thoughts. Then when they left because they could no longer cope with her insecure thinking, it confirmed that she was right to think this way, that it had served her well and proved her right. It also served to reinforce the fact that all men would abandon her, so all the old thoughts and fears resurfaced when she met someone new and so the cycle continued.

Whether it is the sensitive person, the worrier, the angry person or the insecure person, it is all about believing that their thoughts are fact and reacting to them. I have learnt enough over the years to understand that thoughts mean nothing and only you can bring them to life through identifying with them as the truth.

Paying no attention to your thinking

A lot of sufferers spend all day battling with their thoughts in an attempt to change or suppress them. If only they could learn to pay no attention to their thoughts, then their suffering would cease. But trying to pay no attention to your thoughts can be misinterpreted and become another battle, another technique. I was the same and would now be saying “I am taking no notice of you, you aren’t real and cannot harm me”, but once again I was back in ‘technique’ mode as the truth was I was still fearful and fully identified with the thoughts and wanted them to be gone. Once I truly did not care what thoughts arose, I did not need to repeat any sayings or mantras because their presence neither bothered nor concerned me.

This is why I keep mentioning the word technique as a ‘no, no’ for anything anxiety or thought related. A technique does not mean acceptance of what is; it means suppression, denial and a tool used to control or make something go away. With any thought or emotion, the more you struggle to get rid of it, the more you get of what you don’t want. Not giving attention to your thoughts does not mean trying to suppress them or ignore them, it means opening up and allowing them to arise without identifying with them. I am not saying this is easy initially as we have spent all our lives listening to the inner commentary, believing it to be true and so it can take a little practice and it is only natural to get dragged into believing them from time to time.

When you begin to take your thoughts less seriously, then you are automatically able to let them go as they no longer hold your focus and attention. If your negative thoughts still manage to grab your attention, then there is still some fear and belief in them hanging around. Don’t punish yourself for this, just keep practicing letting them pass on through with as little identification and resistance as possible. Allow yourself not to be concerned about anything you think and understand that the content of your thoughts is not important.

Also, and this is vitally important, don’t think ‘But they are still there despite everything Paul said’. Just remember it doesn’t matter what you think. You are not trying to change your thoughts; you are learning to no longer take your thinking seriously. When you let go of giving your attention and belief towards a negative thought, then its fuel is pulled and in time it will fade into nothingness. This is the way to be free of negative/intrusive thoughts; it will never come through trying to change or suppress them.

Only when I allowed myself to think anything without taking it seriously was I truly free. Initially, my thoughts did not change and the old fearful and insecure thinking would still arise due to my brain going through the process of repeating old patterns, but I was no longer bothered or thrown by this and I no longer acted on them. Without my attention and respect and without me struggling with them, they had no fuel to survive and eventually just disappeared. As time went on, my old conditioned thinking was replaced with new fresh thinking. What returned was my natural default thinking, the thought system that was there to serve me well and guide me in life. I had never lost that fresh thinking; it was just temporarily covered up.

Don't fear your thoughts

Imagine a dog that has been abused and even after being taken on by a new caring owner is still petrified of everyone who walks past him in the street because he still believes that all people are out to harm him. So, to keep safe, he will try to avoid all human contact, pull away and hide behind his owner even though these people are not a threat to him.

This avoidance is never going to cure the dog of his fear. He needs to learn over time that these people are totally harmless and only then can they walk past him without him having a fearful reaction. If another dog were across the road, he would have shouted, "Don't worry, these people are harmless. Chill out and enjoy your walk". That's what I would shout to someone who fears their intrusive thoughts. "Don't worry, those thoughts are not real and cannot harm you, just smile at them and enjoy your day".

Yet previously I did the opposite with my thoughts, I believed they were scary, harmful and fact, so I spent years trying to fight, avoid and suppress them. I bought all the pointless books on how to think positive when all I had to learn to do was have a different relationship with them; then and only then would I be at peace with my thinking.

So apart from the pointless and exhausting effort itself, any attempt to prevent or deny thoughts that arise just creates conflict in the mind and is entirely futile. Any thoughts that arise will disappear by themselves if they are not accepted or pursued as the truth. To consciously and deliberately try to erase thoughts is like trying to clean your kitchen floor with dirty water – utterly pointless and counterproductive.

Your thoughts are not who you are

I have added this final conversation I had with someone as I have never seen anyone experience such a shift as quickly as when I said what I did below. To get something from it, you have to not only read the words but really see the truth behind them.

Someone recently contacted me because he was having thoughts about no longer loving his wife and these thoughts really bothered him. He said he was sure he loved her, but maybe he should leave her and finished the conversation off with "I really don't know why I think this way because deep down I'm sure I do love her".

I said "That final statement should tell you everything you need to know. And that is that it is not you that is doing the thinking. Who is that person questioning why you think this way? That illustrates the fact that your thinking is separate from you. It is something that happens within you, but it's not you. So, you are the one who can decide to take these thoughts seriously or not. You can decide whether or not to follow your dysfunctional thinking and let it control you, or you can smile at it and take your own path".

He sent me an email later and said he was no longer identifying with his thoughts. He could see the lie behind them now. He could not understand why there had been such a shift in his thinking. The same thought came up, yet it seemed so silly now and he realised that he loved his wife more than anything. He said "I can't believe a thought made me question leaving her and you're right, I did have a choice to take my thinking seriously or not. Before I just saw it as the truth, maybe because I have done so for 50 years!! But it seems obvious to me now that thoughts are not reality and they are just something that appear; only we can make them appear real. As you mentioned in a previous session, I was stressed at the time, my mood was low and so was my thinking. I was blaming my wife for my misery when it had nothing to do with her. When our mood is low, so is our thinking, and when it is high, the opposite is true, yet nothing in the outside world ever changes. Just seeing this has helped me to no longer take my thoughts seriously - thank you".

So, remember: *Thinking is not the problem; you can think whatever you wish. It is identifying with your thoughts and seeing them as fact, which causes the suffering and stops you living the life you wish.*

Chapter 7

The Inner Critic

If you put belief into any thoughts that you're unworthy, insecure or unlovable, then you're going to walk around with that label. You will then start playing the part, acting it out and losing sight of who you truly are while ruining your interactions with others, denying your own worth and destroying your confidence. The truth is we are all exactly the same. No one is any better than anyone else and therefore it is only our thoughts about ourselves that are different. Once we understand the false nature of these thoughts and no longer put belief into them, then who we think we are starts to fall away and we begin to realise that we are not the story our mind made up about ourselves.

A lot of people struggle with that inner critic; that inner voice that says things like 'you will never amount to anything; you're worthless; no one can love you; you're not interesting enough'. The list of things the mind can come up with to put us down is endless. This inner voice is mainly created through a person's past experiences and interactions. It can be built and strengthened by what our parents, ex-partners, school bullies or even friends have said to us in the past. We create a story and then identity ourselves based on these past experiences. If you have ever come across the word 'ego' in spiritual teachings, then this is what it is. The ego is a thought structure that you take on to be who you are. If you want this negative story to end, then you have to stop putting belief into it.

Unfortunately, most don't do this; they tend to start looking outside of themselves for validation and reassurance. You only have to look on Facebook and social media for evidence of this. You can literally see how someone views themselves through how they use social media.

Have you ever met certain people who you and others really like, yet they do not see this and always think negatively of themselves no matter how many compliments they receive? The point is they are taking their own thoughts about themselves more seriously than the obvious views of others; this is how powerful and believable their thoughts can be. They have built up their own false story about themselves and now believe it to be who they truly are.

A lot of people with anxiety may not have had anyone put them down, and they may have been quite confident people with not much of a story before anxiety became part of their lives. But once they begin to suffer, then their own story can start to develop. They begin to feel weaker than others and their confidence becomes eroded through them not being as sociable and as outgoing as before. They begin to feel they have failed in some way and that no one will want them. They may worry that their partners will get fed up and move on or that they will lose their job and friends. They begin to feel pretty despondent about themselves and their situation and in this depressed and self-critical state, the inner voice can start to go into overdrive.

The only reason this story continues is that they are putting so much belief into it and agreeing with it. They are feeding it on a daily basis through adding even more negative thoughts about themselves, and so the story continues to become more solid and believable. The story can also heighten or lessen with your mood. When we feel at our worst, then the inner critic seems to put us down even more. When we find ourselves in a better mood, then the voice can be almost silent or on rare occasions tell us how great and lovable we are. This ever-changing story again shows us that there is no truth in this personal thought structure; that which keeps changing can never be real.

We always see life through our current perception of ourselves and not how it truly is. When I was at my worst, I thought friends would no longer want to spend time with me; my partner would leave and that I was no longer interesting. My inner critic went into overdrive and I believed every word it said. I know now that it was nonsense and not one person left my side or thought any worse of me. It was all just a reflection of what I thought of myself at the time and not reality.

There is a story about a man called Sydney Banks who went to see a psychiatrist when he felt extremely low and down on himself. He sat there and told him all about his problems and how extremely insecure he was feeling at the time. When he had finished, the psychiatrist just said: "I have never heard such nonsense in all my life". He then said, "Syd you are not insecure, you just think you're insecure". This statement blew Syd away and he instantly saw the truth behind it. He said: 'It was only the belief in my insecure thoughts that created my insecure feelings, but in reality, it did not exist. It was like a bomb going off in my head and was so enlightening it was unbelievable'.

When I read this, it made complete sense to me. Others may not grasp straight away what that means and have such an enlightening experience, but to me, it took me back to my own suffering and how I labelled myself socially awkward when in reality I never truly was. I just put belief into the thoughts that I had nothing interesting to say, that others did not like me and because I believed in these thoughts, then I played my role perfectly, and through playing this role, it reinforced my belief that this was who I was.

I would hide away in the background. I stopped having an opinion, made excuses not to go out, rushed and avoided conversations and all these actions came from putting belief into these thoughts and then acting on them. I am not saying I was great socially at the time, as I wasn't, but me putting this label on myself and believing this is who I was, made me ten times worse. I began to realise that who I thought I was, was nothing more than a bunch of thoughts and old beliefs creating my identity.

Here is another famous Buddhist saying, 'No self, no suffering'. This does not mean to attempt to disappear and no longer exist; it just means don't take the false thought created self seriously, find out who you really are behind it.

How a different view can get rid of suffering in an instant

The following is also a true story. Forgive me for not remembering the names of those involved, as it has been a while since I came across this story, but it was a meeting between a lady and a well-respected health professional in America. This lady came to see him and explained how she had spent the last 25 years in therapy and got nowhere.

She felt so low, had little to no confidence in herself and felt such hatred towards her mother, who she blamed for the mess she was in. She said she loathed herself and thought she was worthless and unlovable. The story was that her mother, who was an alcoholic and in an abusive relationship, had told her as a child that she was useless, ugly and wished she had never been born. All of this had deeply affected her throughout her adult life. All the other therapists she had seen previously had dug up her past and tried to unravel it all piece by piece. This particular therapist did not work like that and said, "Why would I want to bring something painful back up for you to relive it all over again? All I will say is that what your mother said to you had nothing at all to do with you, nothing whatsoever. It could have been your next-door neighbour or the girl you work with and she would have behaved exactly the same towards them too.

The truth is she said these hurtful things to you due to her own pain and suffering. This is why she drank, to hide and suppress what she was feeling, but it wasn't enough to block out what she was going through, there was more pain, and unfortunately, she took that pain out on you. Your mother must have been suffering terribly to speak to you this way and you, unfortunately, got the brunt of her pain. I am not saying what she did and said was right; it was not. But that is why she said those horrible things. Telling you that you were unlovable, stupid or ugly was her way of relieving her own pain and suffering. It was just a reflection of what she thought of herself and was in no way personal".

The woman looked at him and burst into tears. She came back a week later and said "I have been through therapy for 25 years and you have done more for me in that one session than the others did in all that time. Not only has a big weight been lifted from my shoulders, but I also now see that I am not those things she said I was. I don't agree with what she put me through, but for once, I can see why. I even have a little sympathy for my mother and a lot of that hate I felt towards her has now gone".

This woman had built up her own story from her mother's words and her inner critic got hold of the story and reinforced it. All it took was for her to put a different perspective on things thanks to the therapist's words. The way she thought about herself then shifted entirely and with that her inner critic's voice was pretty much silenced.

You can relate this story to any situation. Let's use the ex-partner who told someone they were useless, stupid and that no one would ever want them. Again, like the woman's story above, these cruel words had nothing to do with them and everything to do with the ex-partner's own pain and insecurity. Does it make it right? No, but it sure takes all the emphasis away from the victim and tells them that is not who they are and that they are just the victim of someone else's pain and insecurity. When that abusive partner moves on to the next person, they will more than likely get the same treatment as it was never personal and all to do with the perpetrator.

When a person is treated this way, they can either believe it is all down to them and then the inner critic will reinforce this and tell them it's all true and that the other persons cruel words were right and they are unlovable and useless. Or they can silence that voice by recognising that it was nothing to do with them and everything to do with the person that put them through this. When someone is horrible or nasty to you, it is always a reflection of their own pain and what's going on inside them, so never take it personally and don't put it into the story you create about yourself. Not one person on this planet is any better or more important than the other. We are all exactly the same and only by creating a false story about yourself can this perception change.

The same is true of people who may have become famous, rich or have been told that they are wonderful all their life and so they have thoughts of being more important than others. Some people can become very entitled and start to believe they are better than others and look down on certain people. This sort of behaviour then starts to repel others who may say things like "Who do they think they are?" This is because we all know that at our core, we are all the same; no one is any better or worthier than anyone else. Having thoughts of being better than anyone else is as false as believing you are not as good as others, and both can be equally as damaging.

Silencing the inner critic

Even after gaining a better understanding, the inner critic (the mind) can still try to put you down by repeating old thought patterns. Again, the best way to silence its voice is not to identify with it and know that your story about yourself has no truth in it. The less you identify with these thoughts, the more they begin to fall away and no longer influence your reality.

A lot of people try to silence this inner critic by reading affirmations about how great they are, how people's opinions don't matter and how they need no one but themselves etc. As I said before, I have never been a fan of affirmations as all you get is a ten second boost, but then it's not long before the old thoughts and insecurities come back. If you take no notice of this self-created, false inner critic, then its voice is quietened. It needs your full attention and belief in it to feed its existence. So, the best way to silence the inner critic is to realise it's not in any way fact and stop putting belief into it. Just see it for what it is, which is a mind-made construction of old beliefs and past experiences that hold no truth whatsoever and have nothing to do with who you truly are.

Here is a story that I use that seems to work very well to get my point across. At some point in our life, we have all come across that drunken man with a beer in his hand who shouts obscenities in the street. Well, imagine if when you walked past this man, he started yelling obscenities at you, telling you that you are a useless piece of crap, son of a gun etc. The chances are that you would just ignore him and carry on with your day. You would realise that he didn't mean it and that there is no truth in what he was saying, so it would not affect or bother you in any way. Well, treat your inner critic in exactly the same way. See it as that drunken man shouting utter nonsense. It's not the truth and has no bearing on who you truly are, so smile and just carry on with your day and this inner voice that previously punished you will begin to die out of its own accord.

Chapter 8

Overworking the Brain

(In this chapter I talk about the brain and the mind, the mind being the thinking part of the brain)

A lot of people have mentioned to me that their thoughts tend to race and they often feel detached from their surroundings. They also complain that they can't think straight, they struggle to concentrate, and that even simple tasks seem like such an effort. The problem here is they have given their brains so many projects, worries and concerns to deal with; it is no wonder it ends up so busy, exhausted, fragile and unable to concentrate on any one task. Basically, it is being overworked and this is the reason it is unable to function properly. Are you going crazy? Absolutely not, but you need to stop feeding more projects and worries into that overworked brain and give it a chance to settle down and go back to its natural resting state. Then and only then will clarity and normal thinking return.

Pretty much everyone who comes to me has been stressing and worrying about one situation or another. This continuous stressful thinking has then resulted in them feeling the way they do. The trouble is that, in many cases, they are no longer stressing and overthinking about the initial problem, but more about how they are now feeling. They are constantly worrying, analysing and going over things to try and find a way out of their current state. They are stuck inside their own head, unable to think of anything else but the subject of themselves and how to get better. It is like a puzzle they feel must be worked out before they can be free. So many people fall into this trap without even realising it.

Some may read this book and then keep going over everything I have said, turning it into the next project for their brain to get stuck into, DON'T! You will just exhaust it even further. Please don't ever turn my words into a method, technique or something to constantly carry around with you. They are just a pointer for you to see something so that you no longer do the things that are causing you so much suffering. There really is no method or technique to be had here, just something to see. I had to explain this to someone recently who asked: "Paul, how do I get my mind to settle?" I replied: "By realising that the answers to your problems will not be sorted out through more thinking, you need to put your mind down and then it will settle naturally".

Consequences of overworking the brain

Oh, that poor old brain that is burdened with so many questions and problems to solve, day in day out, from the anxiety sufferer. They search and search in there for answers, yet the answers never come. Do they leave it alone once they can't find the answers they are looking for? No such luck; this poor, exhausted brain is pounded for more solutions to their so-called problems each day, which only leads to it being more exhausted and worn out than ever.

When I suffered, I felt mentally worn out; I felt detached and could not think straight. My mind raced, obsessed over anything and everything and I found it very hard to concentrate on the simplest of tasks. I even found it hard to be in my own company at times and felt the need to constantly escape from myself through sleep or distractions. Yet, what did I do? I went back to the very place that was causing the problem and wore it out even further. My mental health was really suffering due to this cycle, but at the time I did not realise what the problem was, and just when my brain needed a huge break to heal, I worked it even harder. It makes utter sense to me now why the harder I fought and the more I tried to think my way better, the worse things got.

The question I continually pounded my mind with looking for a solution was 'How do I get rid of my suffering?'

My mind said, 'The answer does not lie up here, the answer lies with you, as you are the one creating it. If you want me to function as I did before, then please leave me alone so I can get on with my real purpose in life'.

The only reason a person with anxiety ends up mentally exhausted is because they refuse to feel how they do. They exert immense mental energy, fighting, suppressing and figuring out new ways to manage, avoid or get rid of their suffering. The brain never stops working and so it starts to become exhausted and, in many cases, breaks down. People aren't aware of this self-created cycle and so spend even more mental energy trying to fix this new symptom of mental exhaustion by indulging in more thinking, worrying and struggle, and so it gets worse.

Can you now see why this fighting/suppressing/obsessing approach does not work? The person is again creating their own suffering. Yet most people think the suffering is created outside of themselves and so they need to find something or someone to make it go away.

An overworked brain is a poor servant

Your brain works far better as a machine when it has nothing extra to chew on. Then it can efficiently do the job for which it was designed. Left alone, the mind will come up with far more solutions than when we try to find an answer. Scientists and inventors have stated that their best ideas came to them when they stopped trying to solve a problem. Even when writing this book, I had to take breaks; otherwise, ideas and insights just stopped coming to me. My brain needed a time out to refresh. After a few hours break, ideas would start flowing again. During my days of suffering, all my best insights came to me when I wasn't looking for them and the more my mind cleared, then the more I saw. When I searched for answers, I found them pretty impossible to find, but when I stopped searching these moments of inspiration popped up all the time. When people feel clarity and a break in their suffering for the first time, it is amazing how much wisdom starts coming through.

When your brain feels out of control

Because of all this searching, all this extra workload and the numerous problems you have given your brain to solve, you can start to feel as though it has, shall we say, taken on a mind of its own. It feels like you have lost control over it, and it is now just running wild. You find it hard to think straight; you obsess easily and find it hard to concentrate. Basically, it has lost its resilience and seems to take you where it wishes rather than where you want to go. It seems to have taken on a life of its own and taming it and getting it to do what you want now seems impossible. Instead of it being your servant, it now appears to have turned into your master.

But is it any wonder it is like this? It has been worked way beyond its capabilities and has lost sight of its purpose. It was only there to help and guide you through life; it did not sign up for all of this. It can't take on all these extra worries and work you burden it with, so it starts to run amok. But, like you, it just wants to go back to being your servant. It wants to achieve calm just as much as you do.

Yet it is at this point that people think there is now something wrong and they have to fix this wild and untamed mind. So, where do they go to fix this? Yup, that's right, they go right back into their mind for answers. They are trying to fix their tired, weary and overworked brain with their tired, weary and overworked brain and, well, I think by now you know the result of this. Yes, another never-ending cycle has been created. So much poor mental health is created by this loop and the more people try to fix it, the poorer their mental health becomes.

I had my big aha moment one day when I was in my kitchen making dinner. As usual, I was trying to mentally fix myself because my brain was exhausted and my mind was running wild. I was stood there trying to fix and calm my mind through the process of more thinking and analysing and the only thing I accomplished was to make it worse. It then hit me that the actual process of trying to calm my mind through more thinking and analysing was the reason my mind was becoming more frantic and busier and my brain was becoming more fatigued.

It was never going to heal this way. It didn't need or want more thinking and analysing. It just needed to be left alone in order to finally heal, and that meant just allowing it to be exhausted without the need to constantly try and fix it or sort it out. It came to me so clearly that in trying to fix the problem, I was exhausting my brain further. How had I not seen this before? I was actually creating the fire that I was trying to extinguish. On seeing this, I recognised the obvious loop I was stuck in. I fell into the old trap of thinking that if I did not feel great, then I must be doing something wrong and I had to find a way to fix it, not realising that it was this very action that was keeping me in this loop.

The most important lesson I learnt was that you cannot fix your mind with your mind; it just becomes more out of control. The mind cannot fix the mind any more than it can fix a broken leg or heal a cut finger. It is an intelligence far beyond the mind that does this, and it will do the same here.

The only way your mind will settle is by being left alone. In trying to fix your mind with your mind, you are trying to solve the problem with the problem. This is a very important statement that becomes obvious when grasped. Most people completely miss this important point and spend all their life trying to solve their problems by constantly thinking and analysing all day. They fear that if they don't continue with this, then the answers will never come. A lot of people find it very hard to let go of this constant questioning and searching. They feel that if they do, then they will somehow lose control, when in reality, the opposite is true.

So how do we calm an unruly mind?

Trying to get the mind to do what you want is like trying to tie a horse to a pole. It will jump and buck and become unrulier than ever, make more noise and become even more distressed. You are far better setting it free to run around where it wishes. This is the only way to tame the mind is to leave it be; it cannot be done by force.

When my overworked mind started to obsess and run amok, I likened it to an unruly child having a tantrum. I had previously tried to control it, reason with it, fix it, tell it off and argue with it, but it never seemed to settle. Once I gave up and let the mind run around and do as it wished, it just seemed to settle on its own, which, of course, now makes complete sense.

Regaining clarity through understanding

As you may have now gathered, there is a very simple explanation as to why you feel the way you do. Your brain is being overworked, which is the reason why you may feel restless, irritable and struggle to think clearly, as well as having racing thoughts and certain obsessions. Reducing the brain's workload is the key to regaining a healthy and obedient mind. But the reason most people are unable to reduce it is that they look to the very thing that is causing the problem and hike up the mind's activity even further and so the brain never gets the rest it so craves to heal itself. So many miss this point and spend all their time using their mind to try and sort out their problems, by worrying, attempting to fix and constantly analysing how they feel.

I cannot stress enough how you now need to leave the mind alone to heal and allow all of this past momentum to ebb away. While doing so, you will still feel as though your mind is all over the place and it may still act up for a while but, don't worry; this is entirely normal. In order for the momentum to subside, you just have to allow your mind to go through any movement it wishes and for as long as it takes. If it wants to be noisy, then let it be noisy. If it wants to obsess, then let it obsess. If it wants to throw a bunch of crazy thoughts around, then let it. Don't fight with your mind, all you will achieve is to mentally fatigue yourself and make it even busier.

To allow the past momentum of the mind to ebb away you must be totally at one with its movement and not try to control or tame it in any way. Just leave it to go through its own process, whatever that entails, and when left alone it will then begin to sort itself out. This does take a lot of trust at times because when it feels out of control and starts having some kind of tantrum, your instinct will be to try to do something about it, to put a leash on it. But, trust me if you keep struggling with it, all this will do is keep you in a loop.

I remember once going to bed and my mind was all over the place, thinking of this and that and, as usual, I got involved. I reasoned with it, got annoyed with it, got involved with its stories and tried to think of something else, yet it just carried on with its inner chatter and noise. As I was tired, entirely out of the blue, I just said, 'OK, you can do what you want, I am off to sleep'. And just like that, because my attention was taken away from it and I left it alone, it then settled and I more or less went straight off to sleep. This really surprised me, and it gave me an insight into the fact that my mind could run as wild as it wanted, but I did not have to get annoyed or involved with it. It was my fault it had reached this frantic, worn-out stage anyway, so it wouldn't be fair to get angry with it, it just needed my love and care now, not my fury.

Feeling mentally blocked

This is something else people mention to me. Apart from their minds, seemingly running amok, they also say that they feel mentally blocked. It is like their mind feels so congested that they find it hard to think straight. They may also find it an effort to follow a conversation, or when they read something, the words are not sinking in.

Rather than this being a constant worry cycle, it is more of an information-gathering cycle where people just go from one technique, website and book to another, trying to find the answers they so crave. It is a never-ending cycle of information gathering which this over-stuffed mind is going to have to process and then find some non-existent space to store it. Just when it tries to have a clear-out and refresh itself, here comes some more information and so it continues to feel blocked and unresponsive.

This is why people say they need a break when they have done too much studying or work that involves a lot of concentration. They may even come home and complain that their mind is still whirring away or full of all the work they have done that day. When they take a break, their mind is able to step back and process and release all the information it has received that day. It is like a vacuum cleaning a dirty carpet. After the much-needed break, their mind is refreshed and clear, and they are able to go back the next day and work at their optimum level again. The anxiety sufferer never heeds these signs to take a break and continues to feed in more and more information. Can you see now why the mind can feel so blocked, detached, irritable and why you feel so mentally worn out?

This is something I went through too. It took me a long time to finally learn how to get out of this state as everyone I went to see and every book I read would just give me another technique to try or another mantra to repeat. I would then have a bunch of rules/sayings to remember and carry around with me. Talk about weighing me down and working the mind even harder!! Looking back, no person or book ever gave me a direct answer to this problem. I basically had to figure it out for myself by coming to my own realisations and having a better understanding of how the brain works.

Understanding mental congestion

The brain works just like the body, and when there is not enough mental space for it to cope with what you are feeding it, it then begins to feel full and congested. Your stomach tells you when it has had enough; you feel the sensation of being full and so stop eating. Your brain does the same, but you don't listen and carry on stuffing it with more information, more problems to solve and then wonder why it feels so full and why you struggle to process any more information. This is why I am forever telling people to leave the subject behind and go out and live their life.

Because your body can't speak, it sends its messages through emotions and it is up to us to listen and understand what it is telling us. It makes sense that if your brain feels heavy and blocked and there seems to be no room to think, that you are overworking it and feeding it more information than it can cope with. These emotions don't pick on you; they are always pointing out to you that something is wrong and that change is needed. When you feel that your brain is blocked and congested, it is telling you exactly that. If it could speak it would say 'Hang on buddy, give me a break. Don't give me anything more to chew on'.

Every home computer has a different capacity for storing information and you can keep adding programs and files until this space is filled. When it is almost full, it will start to slow down and become sluggish (ring a bell?). Once it has reached its full capacity, the computer will tell you that there is no more disk space available and you then have to clear it so that it can function at its optimum level. Your brain works in the same way and can automatically clear this disc space if left alone to do so. Unfortunately, when you keep feeding it more and more information, it never gets the chance. It is trying to tell you something, but you are not listening.

At one time, I felt so flat, half-baked and detached that I figured that there was something wrong with me and so I had to fix myself. So, I thought more, read more and analysed more, but all this did was feed more and more information into my already overworked brain. The mental effort I put into trying to feel better just exhausted me further. I woke up and the whole day was built around finding answers. Even reading this back makes me wonder why I never 'got it' at the time; it seems so obvious to me now. I really had no idea that it was this mental exhaustion and a lack of mental space that had me feeling this way. Because of the way I was approaching this, it's any wonder why I felt flat, exhausted, clogged up and struggled to read a book or why I felt like hiding away and found it so difficult to engage in conversations.

I repeat, this is why you don't need to do anything, as it is the doing that causes the problem. You don't have to do anything, but you do have to see the truth behind why you feel the way you do. An understanding or insight beats any pill or technique hands down. Once I had this understanding, it was the end of this never-ending cycle. I still felt mentally blocked and exhausted for a while due to everything I had put my brain through previously, but now that I understood it and so this feeling no longer worried or concerned me. Without all that extra worry and concern or need to solve or fix this problem, my brain started to heal, my mind began to clear and I began to experience moments of real clarity.

The brain is the same as any muscle that is pushed beyond its limits; eventually, you will feel the pain of overworking it. The only cure is to rest it. It may still ache for a while, but once you stop overusing it, then your body's healing system will take over and repair the damage. You cannot force a muscle to stop aching by using it more, just as I could not force my mind to clear through more thinking and analysing.

I look back to my days of suffering and all I did every day was live in my head. If I wasn't analysing my condition, I was reading about it. If I wasn't worrying about my state, I was trying to fix it. I had no timeouts, no mental breaks and the more exhausted, clogged up and detached I felt, the more I continued to do the above and so the cycle of exhaustion continued.

If you want your mind to settle and your brain to become less sluggish and tired, then stop stuffing more and more information into it by way of rules, techniques, Googling, reading and analysing.

The mind has a brilliant way of calming and righting itself if left alone to do so and the brain can overcome any exhaustion; they need no intervention from you. This shows that you never lost anything and were always there beneath your current state. You have perfect mental health by default and that part of you is untouchable. You can go away from it at times, but it is always there ready to be accessed once again.

You just need to know how.

Chapter 9

Avoiding Anxiety

Avoiding anxiety, otherwise known as avoidance coping, is when someone tailors their behaviour to try and escape particular thoughts and feelings. If you want to stay in the cycle of anxiety, then this is a pretty good way to go about it. No one knows this better than I do, as I was the master of this behaviour. In fact, very few people who come to me for help don't do this in one form or another.

The trouble with avoidance techniques is that they may work in the short term, but in the long-term, they create more of the very feelings people are trying to escape from and can also train our mind to falsely believe that the outside world is a scary place to engage in.

Examples of avoidance

Not answering the phone

Spending an excessive amount of time watching TV

Constantly cancelling on people

Turning to alcohol or food

A need to be busy or distracted

Excessive exercise

Isolating oneself

Fabricated conversations

Gambling

Living your life online

Avoiding the outside world

The cost of avoiding your feelings

Constantly exhausted/drained

A detrimental effect on personal relationships

A decline in overall health

Loss of confidence

Continued suffering

Smiling on the outside while crying on the inside

Explosions of anger or frustration

Feeling Irritable

Wearing a mask in front of others

Not living the life you want

Feelings of depression

The best way to free yourself of anxiety or any uncomfortable emotion is to fully allow yourself to experience it. To transcend suffering, we need to feel the very feelings we are trying to avoid. The paradox is that being prepared to feel and experience anxiety will, in the long run, lead to less anxiety. This also means that you no longer avoid going places where your anxiety may rise. In doing so, you are teaching your mind that this anxious response is no longer needed while allowing any stored up anxious energy to be released.

It wasn't until I wrote down the list of things I was doing to avoid that I finally saw how much of life I was still missing out on. Some of mine were subtle, some not so. Once I wrote them down, I decided that I would no longer build my life around avoiding certain feelings and emotions. Some temporary discomfort was far better than long term avoidance that was getting me nowhere. All this approach achieved was to restrict my life to such a degree that I barely had one, and I refused to live this way any longer.

It took me quite a while before I realised that the reading of self-help books, taking medication, the Googling of symptoms and seeking out counsellors were all down to avoidance of feelings. I wanted these books, internet searches, pills and counsellors to make it all go away and when they failed, I looked elsewhere. The problem was I was looking in the wrong direction, as nothing on the outside could make these feelings go away. The only thing that anyone outside of me could do to help was to point me in the right direction to finally allow myself to experience them, yet very few did. They just made me even more convinced that this was me forever and only passed on more methods/techniques to help me manage how I was feeling and not get to the root cause that could have freed me for good.

No one ever said to me "Hey Paul, the way out of all this is very simple; just go towards and willingly feel all that you have been avoiding so far. Don't spend all your life trying to avoid, suppress or get rid of these feelings. They just need space to be felt and released". No, I got the opposite advice: 'Do this, try this, read that, take this. Yes, these emotions are bad; let's go on a mission to get rid of them'. If I only knew then what I know now!

Suffering is caused by resistance to what is

What a lot of people fail to understand is that around 20% of suffering is due to the particular emotion you are experiencing and 80% is caused by your resistance towards it. It is the resistance to how you are feeling that creates the greatest suffering.

Most people are afraid to truly experience their feelings. They are afraid of the discomfort involved in feeling their emotions and also falsely believe that if they allow them, then they will somehow take them over. So, they end up in a never-ending battle of trying to escape or suppress how they feel. People may drink, take drugs, exercise excessively or go on shopping sprees - anything to avoid feeling what needs to be felt. But going down this road will bring nothing but a lifetime of suffering, as all of these suppressed emotions have nowhere to go and so they just carry on building up inside you, creating more problems. You can only run away, drink and suppress for so long before things start to creak.

What if I no longer attempt to feel any different than I do?

When you feel positive emotions, you don't start questioning them by asking, "Why do I feel good? Why don't I feel bad? I must change my state of mind; this isn't right!' So, if you don't question and try and change things when you feel good, then why do it when you feel bad? Trust me; if you started to create resistance over good feelings, then it would not be long before you started to suffer. Any kind of resistance will bring on suffering as you are going against what is, and in doing so, creating so much internal conflict. It is this internal conflict, this battle for things to be different than they are, that causes the majority of your suffering and depletes you of so much emotional and mental energy.

I didn't accept my anxious feelings for one minute. I spent years attempting to fight and suppress them. I was forever trying to fight and think my way out of how I was feeling and things just got worse. It was after one particular day of carrying out this pointless battle that I said 'What would happen if I no longer tried to feel any different than I do, what would happen then?' This honestly was the turning point for me; as the battle and all the resistance towards how I was feeling began to fall away.

This was not the end of my suffering by any means as I had a lot of past suffering to heal, but it was the end of my battle with how I was feeling and this in itself brought so much welcome relief, not just emotionally, but mentally too as the very act of constantly fighting and rejecting how I felt required immense mental energy.

You are in a period of your life where you feel anxious; learn for once to accept and allow the fact that you won't always feel great in your current state. If you accept this fact and learn to fall into your suffering instead of fighting against it, then all the suffering from that resistance will fall away.

When you stop battling with how you feel on a daily basis, then a large part of its fuel to recreate is taken away and a door to recovery is opened. By finally letting go of control, all the stored-up emotions and feelings that you have been attempting to suppress for years will finally find an outlet and be released. These emotions have never stopped knocking and were waiting for the day you finally allow their presence.

As you fully let go into how you feel, then you may feel certain emotions even stronger than before. But don't worry as this is entirely normal, it is like finally opening up a dam and all these emotions you have previously fought against and suppressed come rushing forward. This is a good thing; it means you are finally freeing them up instead of wearing yourself out trying to suppress or avoid them. Once you understand this process, then you won't fear any sudden increase in emotions or wonder if something has gone wrong. This increase is actually a good sign, not a bad one; it means you can finally allow yourself to release what has been causing you so much suffering.

Learn to accept yourself as you are

I am not asking you to accept yourself when you feel great; we can all do that. Are you willing to accept yourself as you are now?

In this current moment, this is how you feel. Can you accept this fact? Can you accept this current version of yourself? I am not talking about some futuristic balanced and peaceful version – anybody can accept that. I'm talking about this unbalanced, fearful and messy version you are currently experiencing, the one you have been fighting with for so long.

Forget about becoming free one day. Instead, take this current version of "you" and show it your full love and acceptance. This 'you' is not 'you' forever, but while it is, learn to live in peace alongside it and surrender to it, this is where real change happens.

Even now, beyond my suffering, I can have rare days where I feel down, encounter some negative thinking and it truly does not bother me. It hardly touches me as I have not labelled it as bad and spent all day trying to change or escape how I feel. Consequently, my day is not full of resistance and inner conflict and so I don't create any extra suffering. Everything is as it is, and without me struggling against my experience then in return, my mood improves far quicker. It's just like a storm passing over. I accept it's going to rain at some point in my life, but I know it will soon pass and the sun will always come back out.

In the past, when it rained, I would spend all day trying to push the rain back into the clouds. I would think "No, I don't want to feel like this; go away". If that did not work, I would paint on my smile and pretend to the outside world that everything was great, which was so exhausting and just ended up making me feel far worse. I ended up feeling like some kind of fake fraud, which I was, as that's not how I was truly feeling. It was as though I convinced myself that if I act happy, then I might feel it, but all I was doing was denying how I felt and putting another mask on. Now if I feel a bit down, I accept it. I won't apologise for it or try to feel any different. All my masks are now in the bin and it's a very liberating feeling.

So now if it's raining, so what, full stop. For once in my life I am open to feeling both positive and negative emotions, I am human after all and it is amazing how much lighter you feel when you finally allow yourself to just go with the flow of your emotions.

Me hitting rock bottom is what saved me

When I had tried everything to feel better and nothing had worked, I finally hit a brick wall, there was nowhere else to go, nothing left to try and I felt so defeated. I had tried every book, counsellor and technique that I had come across and nothing had made any real difference. It was at this point I concluded there was no way out and this was my life now. It was only when I bottomed out that I realised I had one option left and this was to just surrender to how I was feeling; to no longer try to battle, suppress or run away from it.

It was the only thing I had left. In fact, bottoming out was the best thing to happen to me as I finally realised that I was on the wrong path all along. I had been on this pointless path for years and, along the way, I had found nothing but more suffering. Yet within this suffering, I had found everything. I had found that the real answer was the opposite of what I thought it was. Without going through every so-called cure and failing, without spending years struggling and getting nowhere, I would never have finally given up.

I only stopped searching when there was nowhere else to search; I only stopped battling when I was utterly defeated. It was like I had to go through all this to realise it was all a waste of time. All along my mind and body were telling me to surrender, to give up this pointless battle with myself and until I took heed of this message, my suffering continued.

It seemed too simple at first as my mind still wanted a technique, a saying or belief to hang on to, so as to escape my suffering. I finally saw through this endless loop and realised all this had been the problem all along; I just needed to finally leave myself alone and allow my mind and body to go through its own healing process.

Someone once said to me 'When I first read your book, I put it to one side because it wasn't giving me a technique and so I moved on to find something else. But when I ran out of places to search and things to try, I started to realise the truth in what you had been saying and no matter what else I read, something always drew me back to your words. It was like some inner guidance telling me that here was the real answer'.

We all have our techniques or strategies not to feel something that we deem to be negative. We are always taught that feeling bad must be eliminated. This is why you often see new life coaches, gurus and the latest technique pop up. We see pictures of people selling the idea of happiness with a painted smile and a promise of being just like them for a mere $500. Like they hold some kind of secret, only it will cost you a small fortune to find it out.

When someone asks us how we are, even if we feel awful, we tend to say we are fine. A lot of people feel the need to post positive stories on social media, portraying a false image of how great their lives are. It is as though we feel we have to keep up a pretence to the outside world that we never get down or have problems.

Can't we drop all this and just allow ourselves to feel how we are feeling and not be ashamed to do so? The irony of this is that when we do, we start to feel so much better. Trying to keep any act up is exhausting. When we are not continually trying to change or manufacture our experience or put on pretences for others, then the constant struggle with ourselves ends and peace of mind and balance starts to occur naturally.

I have never been at a better point in my life than I am now and none of it came through trying to deny anything or change my current mood. It was only when I stopped trying to deny how I felt and fully embraced who I was that real change happened. My mind and body found its own balance without any attempt at manipulation from me; just like all of nature finds balance when left alone. Peace and happiness are not something you can force or manipulate; they are your natural state. So, stop trying to be happy, stop trying to be at peace, allow yourself to feel exactly how you do in this moment and in time a change will happen naturally.

Chapter 10

Resistance Only Increases Suffering

As a follow on from the previous chapter, let's go further into resistance and see the role it plays in so much suffering.

Resistance occurs when we want something to be different than it is; when we want to be somewhere else rather than where we are, or we want to feel different than what we do. This creates a void, and so the battle then starts to try and bridge this gap. I don't want to feel like this, so I'm going to try and feel like that. This is the battle that so many anxiety sufferers go through each day and it was a battle that consumed me. I thought it was my job to get from here to there and to constantly manipulate my experience.

The truth is that you can't control your emotions and you can't control your thoughts. This realisation can eventually lead you to finally surrendering this control. My surrender came through, finally getting to a stage where I was just exhausted with 'trying' to continually control my thoughts and feelings. I had become so utterly worn out with it all that I just gave in. This came with a sense of, 'just come then, I'm done trying to change or deny you, I would rather feel you than be in a constant battle with you each day'. It was only then that I began to feel some peace and started to see the benefits to this attitude and the science behind it.

I loved this short message a lady sent me not too long ago as it showed me that this person had truly got the message.

"Paul, I am so excited, and you were right. This has taken a while, but I have now got it. What I have seen is that when I have all these doubts, insecurities, obsessive thoughts and all the other things that I thought I had to work on separately, if I let them all rise into my awareness without resisting any of them and with no fear of the consequences of doing so, then eventually they just dissolve. It can be quite testing at times and it can feel overwhelming on occasions, but now that I know nothing ever comes of it, I no longer fear the experience and know without a doubt that it will pass. Now I don't even question whether or not this is the right way home; I just know it is and I wanted to say thanks for showing me the way out of all of this".

Again, this lady did not have to do anything but allow herself to experience what she had previously fought against and tried so hard to suppress.

A lot of resistance is caused by fear. Fear of fear itself, fear of thoughts, emotions; of not being able to cope or that you will somehow lose control if you don't attempt to stay on top of everything. If people did not fear their current experience, then so much resistance and suffering would fall away.

It is the avoidance and suppression of any emotion that causes it to build up within your inner space.

Take anger, for example. This is just a form of energy that is felt as an emotion and when the energy has passed, then the anger subsides. Someone who experiences a lot of anger will most likely have been through a lot of negative experiences in their life that has caused this anger to build up. This may come through a lack of love when they were younger, or they may have been bullied or treated badly and didn't have the courage to stand up for themselves and so things steadily built up inside. Pretty much everyone who carries a lot of anger has a story to tell of how this energy was created.

A lot of boxers talk about how they grew up full of anger and got into a lot of fights. When they discovered boxing, all that anger/stored up energy then had another outlet and was now released in a constructive way, whereas the only way it was released before was by exploding at others. This build-up of unresolved anger is the very reason a lot of people end up in prison. If this anger is continually suppressed, then it will keep coming back to the surface until it finds an outlet to be released, which is true of any emotion which has been suppressed.

As I have said before, energy can't be destroyed; it can only ever be released. Whatever the emotion, it just needs to be experienced before it can be released. If the person full of anger can allow this anger to rise up within him without acting on it or find another outlet like boxing, then in time they will be free of this energy and live a far more peaceful life. So, the answer would be to no longer suppress this energy of anger, but also no longer feel the need to express it by blaming anything or anyone outside of them for the way they feel.

The only reason I now feel far more peace in my life is because I have released the anxious energy within me. Previously I spent years unknowingly creating more of it while also attempting to suppress it, and this is why nothing changed.

Releasing emotions is not about allowing them and then hoping they will go away, it is about completely opening up to them without trying to deny, suppress, sort them out or distract yourself from them. It is allowing them to enter your space without trying to hold distance or attempt to change them, regardless of whether or not they are uncomfortable.

When I hear someone say "But how can I not try to change my emotional state when I feel so awful?" I respond by saying "Has attempting to deny it ever worked? It's trying not to feel awful that causes you to feel awful because all you are doing is creating more inner conflict and extra stress. If you just let a feeling or emotion manifest itself and pass on through unhindered, you will be surprised by how much sooner it disappears and how much less effect it has on you.

Feeling good one day then back to square one

Another thing I get asked all the time is "Why do I feel great one week and then awful the next?" This is where a lot of people make a huge mistake. After hearing what I tell them, they think that they should never feel bad again. They may have a few fantastic days and think they have cracked it, but that storm will very likely come back and what do they do? They go into "Oh no, I thought I had cracked this. Why do I feel like this again? What am I doing wrong?" and then they fall back into a cycle of rejecting how they feel once again.

If only they could have reminded themselves that it's just another storm passing over; the mind and body going through another process of healing and more energy being released, then they would not have fallen back into the cycle of denying how they feel. As night is day, emotions are always changing, so just accept this. The anxiety sufferer will have a lot of uncomfortable emotions to deal with as all these energies come up to be released; it won't happen overnight.

So, you do have a choice. You can allow yourself to experience these thoughts and emotions, or you can spend all day in your head trying to suppress or change them. Trust me, I know through experience which one causes the most suffering and keeps you in a constant loop.

When you are able to allow even the most painful, uncomfortable and fearful emotions to arise, over time they WILL dissolve into nothing and peace will be restored.

Chapter 11

Why does life bring so much Suffering?

I used to ask myself this very question, as I always seemed to be in some form of suffering in my adult life. So, during my recovery, I wanted to look deeper into what created my anxiety and discontent in the first place.

Yes, I would have some good days along the way, but I spent most of my time unhappy and always seemed to be worrying about something or other.

Life just always seemed to be against me and wouldn't fall into my ideal; nothing seemed to go right, and people didn't act in the way I wanted or say what I thought they should say.

I was always searching for what was missing while thinking the outside could give it to me and so that's where I looked. I thought, 'I just need that promotion, a new car, a new partner, my own home and then I will finally be happy' yet I achieved most of these things and still peace and happiness eluded me.

I also thought I had to manipulate the world into what I wanted it to be to find peace and happiness. If only I could get others to act how I wanted, then I would finally be OK. I concluded like so many others do that it was the fault of the outside world and others why I was unhappy and that I just needed to make sure the outside and others fell into my idea of how things should be, and then peace of mind and happiness would follow.

This peace of mind and happiness is what everyone is looking for; they aren't looking for the new car as a possession; they are looking for how it will make them feel. But how can a lump of metal ever make you feel happy inside? It can't; it will never fill that lack inside, nothing on the outside can.

I genuinely believe that is why so many people do suffer these days as we are constantly bombarded with how we should look, how much money we should have, what material things we need, what job we require, what kind of relationship we should have. That unless we achieve these things, then we can't be happy. Unfortunately, the consumer market only has one interest, and your inner happiness is not one of them.

I finally realised that finding peace and happiness is an inside job and that the outside may bring snippets here and there, but I won't find true peace and joy out there if I don't already feel it within.

Blaming the outside can harm our friendships and relationships.

Blaming the outside for how we are feeling is also why many friendships and relationships can break down, as we mistakenly blame the other person for our emotional disturbance and unhappiness. Because we blame them for how we are feeling, then we may lash out or think that the answer to our happiness is to change them and this is what ends up causing so much friction and arguments.

We can end up lashing out at others because we genuinely believe that this is what is causing us to feel the way that we do. It is the same with life, if we honestly think that life is making us suffer then we attempt to manipulate it. When this doesn't work, we get angry, frustrated, stressed and so of course we suffer.

You have no control over others

The simple truth is that we have no control over how others act, who they are is hardwired into them and the result of the experiences they have had in life. If they truly aren't the person for you and the majority of their behaviour genuinely does make you unhappy, then in most cases you have the choice to leave the relationship or friendship behind.

But if you genuinely love and care for that person and want more peace and less drama in your friendships and relationships, then begin to accept them as they are. Even if there are little quirks that annoy you then try to recognise that no one is perfect.

Celebrate the fact we are all different; you cannot mould someone into who you want them to be. All attempts will just end up with them resenting you, cause so much conflict and in some cases lead to you losing that person.

In my days of suffering, I lost a couple of relationships and a good friendship, as I too eventually blamed them for how I was feeling, I concluded that if I was suffering, then it had to be them. It was only when I took a break and stepped back that I realised that I was the cause of all the friction and drama and that I was just projecting and blaming the other person for how I was feeling and so the inevitable break up followed.

It was at this point that I realised that I was doing the same thing with life. I was blaming my lack of happiness and inner peace on life itself. I honestly thought my life was the reason I was suffering and so I either spent all my time complaining about it or trying to manipulate it and then getting angry when it wouldn't fall into place.

I would complain when it rained, complain when I was stuck in traffic, moan when the shop ran out of milk, get angry if someone cancelled on me, the list was endless.

The irony is that all of these things that I thought were making me suffer, I didn't have one ounce of control over. Yet, there I was spending my whole day complaining about them!! There were people in the world who had no food, water or transport and could only dream of going to the shop to buy food, to drive a car and be stuck in traffic or have water drop from the sky so they could cure their thirst, and there was I complaining about it all.

I started to understand now that my suffering and my breakdown was not due to life but my non-acceptance of life as it was. It began to make real sense as to why I was always stressed and unhappy. My lack of happiness and peace was due to my complete resistance to life as it was and because of this, my mind was never at peace with anything.

If my mind was always disturbed, stressed, worried and complaining, then it made sense as to why I was never at peace. Life and others didn't need to change to suit me; this was all down to my attitude changing.

Accepting life is full of ups and downs

The end of so much of my suffering was about seeing life and reality as it truly was and making peace with it, even when things didn't go my way. I never complained when life went well, so why would I complain when it didn't? Where was the rule made that it must always go our way?

The truth is that life is full of ups and downs, good and bad things will happen; that is the reality of life. But I never accepted this; life always had to go how I wanted it to, and others must behave how I thought they should. I was at constant war with my experience and then wondered why I suffered as I did! It seems utterly crazy to me now that I could ever believe this was possible and that I could ever think I would find peace with this mindset. The odds of one day going exactly how I felt it should, would be over a billion to one, never mind for the rest of my life.

Life didn't care about me or my needs; it just carried on regardless. I could either accept the reality of life with all its ups and downs or I could spend all my days suffering by fighting, worrying and getting angry with it. I tried the latter approach for many years and life always won; it wouldn't change because I wanted it. I still got stuck in traffic, it continued to rain on my day off, and I still couldn't find my keys when I was late.

I finally accepted that life was a mixture of ups and downs, highs and lows. Some days great things would happen, and other days everything would go wrong. This process was part of life, and the ones who suffer less are the ones who accept this. I used to come across people who always seem to be chilled and calm, nothing seemed to go wrong, and I thought they were just lucky. Looking back now, I realise it had nothing to do with luck; they mainly had the same problems as others, but they just accepted them as part of life. It wasn't life that created their inner calm; it was their attitude towards it.

A true story of how a change in attitude brought less suffering

I have told the story below before, but I think it is worth repeating as it had such an effect on me and taught me a lot about how we create so much of our own suffering.

It is a story about a man who had fought in the gulf war where he had lost a leg and half his arm in combat and was bound to a wheelchair for the rest of his life. He said when he first arrived home, he would argue with everyone around him, snap at his partner and children. He wouldn't accept any help and started drinking heavily. He felt immense frustration and anger due to his situation and what life had thrown at him and fell into a deep depression.

He was on the verge of ending it all until he looked at his daughter sleeping and a sudden realisation hit him. He finally realised he did have so much to live for and that even with his disability, he could still enjoy life. He may not look like he did before, but inside he felt like the same person, and that it was only the anger at his predicament that was changing his personality. He said it was at that moment that he fully accepted his situation and with it, this immense calm came over him. He realised he wasn't suffering because of being in a wheelchair but because he hadn't accepted it.

This man went on to represent his country in the Paralympics and now does talks all over the country to those in similar situations.

This story hit me very hard when I read it, and it took me back to my non-acceptance of my anxiety that created so much extra suffering. When I initially suffered, I was always fighting against it, arguing with it and feeling sorry for myself, not once did I accept my situation. I remember feeling a similar peace when I let go and just allowed myself to fall into it. The anxiety was still there, but it felt different now I had finally allowed its presence and all the extra suffering created through the resistance to it fell away.

The same principle held true for my life, that life wasn't making me suffer; it was my non-acceptance of the ups and downs of it that did. My suffering was telling me that I wasn't accepting life and others as they were.

This realisation is just pure science that if you allow things to be as they are, then there is nothing to stress or worry about, so then only peace remains. I am not saying this is easy at first, especially when we are conditioned to react differently, but with practice, it does start to become a more natural way of being.

My first test of this new attitude came when I was out cycling and had my wallet and phone stolen from my car. Apart from the financial cost, this was a major headache to me as it meant changing all my bank cards, getting a new driving licence and also the hassle of getting a new phone. But even though all this had happened, I was strangely calm, like I had this inner knowing that there was nothing I could do about it. What had happened was the reality of the situation, and there was no point getting stressed or worried about it, all I could do was go and sort it out.

I would not say that I always reacted correctly and at times I did fall back into old responses, but overall there was a real shift in my attitude and due to this I found a lot more inner peace.

Accepting life as it is

Accepting life as it is doesn't mean you don't try and achieve anything, it's good to succeed as long as it is not to the detriment of your health.

It also doesn't mean you shrug your shoulders and stop caring. It means you learn to accept the reality of the situation and then take what action is needed to resolve it in a calm and balanced way - understanding that getting angry and stressed about it only hurts you and does nothing to change the situation.

I know there are things in life that really test us and I recently had a situation where I couldn't help but feel the strain of it. I didn't try and deny this, I accepted the predicament and just did the best I could and allowed the concern to be present while adding no more worry to the mix. I also realise that some really traumatic things have happened to people in their life that have caused them a lot of pain and they may need extra help and support to work through them.

I am mainly reaching out to those who continuously stress and worry over everyday problems, things that they have no control over. To help them see that not one person who has lived on this planet has not had things go wrong. I am not saying this new attitude happens overnight, it doesn't, but life will present you with opportunities every day to practice, and in time the new approach becomes automatic.

It is about training your mind to react differently to a situation, so it spends more time in a calm space and less time in a frantic, worrying state. The less you worry and stress, then the more your mind begins to calm down naturally, and so you start to feel more peace in your life.

So much suffering is self-created

I was the reason I had a breakdown; it wasn't due to my life or circumstances; it was a wrong vision on my part, a non-acceptance of reality as it was. My life didn't need to change for me to be happy and find peace, just my relationship with it.

My suffering was actually telling me this and guiding me back to the right path; it forced me to look and change and so in that sense, it was a blessing.

You can't create peace; as it is your natural state. To experience it, you just need to stop doing the things that are disturbing it. My worrying, complaining and stressing is what took me away from it. You look at anyone who suffers, and in most cases, you will find a chronic worrier, stressor or someone who always expects things to go their way. Life won't fall into place for them to no longer suffer; only a change in attitude and perception will.

Life still brings me the same problems and challenges as it did before, but my reaction and way of dealing with them are entirely different. I no longer spend my time pointlessly complaining or worrying, and due to this, I have much more peace in my life.

Life didn't change to bring me far more peace and happiness, I did.

Chapter 12

Setbacks

The subject of setbacks comes up so often that I decided to cover it again in this book and explain precisely what they are and how they are an essential part of recovery. Too many people falsely believe that unless they feel good all the time, then they must be doing something wrong.

Before we start, I am talking about real setbacks here, not just the usual ups and down we can feel each day because of anxiety - that's natural. Some days it rains and some days the sun shines, everyone's mood shifts from time to time. I am talking about the kind of setback where a person feels a lot of peace and freedom for a period of time, then gets engulfed with a return of all their symptoms, thinking they are back to square one and so mistakenly start to battle and question it all over again.

Each person's version of a setback is different. It can be the return of anxious feelings, depersonalisation or obsessive thoughts to name but a few. It doesn't matter what it is, the advice is always the same, but to save confusion, I will talk mainly about the most common setback and that is the return of anxious feelings.

When I suffered from anxiety, obsessive thinking and all the skewed belief systems that went with it, I did what everyone else tends to do and worried, fought, avoided, suppressed and analysed; basically, everything that was keeping me in the cycle of suffering. When I finally understood this cycle, I then started to just allow these feelings instead of constantly trying to suppress/reject them and things slowly began to change. Yet, one thing always kept me stuck and that was the frustration of the return of my symptoms after a period of freedom.

Let's start with my first true realisation.

I mentioned this insight earlier in the book, but here is a more detailed description of that day. I was walking around stuck in my head, as usual, thinking about me, what was wrong and trying to forcibly change my experience. The world was passing me by and as usual, I felt no part of it. Then just as I was doing my usual mental workout something came to me: "This is clearly not working, what if for today I do not try to change how I feel, how would that work?" I actually found it strange that after years of doing the opposite and getting nowhere, I had never thought of this before. But the mind is a stubborn little machine and if it does not like something, then it will try every trick in the book to try and get rid of it. The words though really came from being utterly fed up of battling with myself, I had just had enough.

Anyway, going back to that day, this is what I decided to do. There would be no analysing, no avoiding and no trying to feel different. Much to my surprise, I felt far better that day. I still had all the thought storms, confusion and anxiety flying around, but it wasn't as heavy and didn't touch me the same. There was a sense of peace wrapped around it, like it was there, but I did not care as much. As I had also stepped out of my head by no longer analysing or trying to change things, I felt far more in touch with the world around me and didn't feel as mentally drained. I was also much more aware of my surroundings and the outside world didn't look so flat and grey.

I was so excited by this that I did it the next day and the same thing happened. I woke with the usual feelings of dread, anxiety and thoughts, but I did nothing about them. I just got up and went about my day and found it much easier; in fact, I felt pretty damn good. At last, I thought, I have cracked this thing. All I had to do was to no longer get involved or try to change my experience and I would feel like this all the time.

Well, this went on for about four days until one day I woke and felt dreadful again. I tried not getting involved, not bothering about how I felt and not analysing, but this time the feelings were too strong. I concluded that I must have been wrong and that what I did was just a coincidence. If not, then it worked for a few days, but no longer. So, I had to face the fact that this was me now. I thought that I was free but, clearly, I was not and I was now stuck with this for good, another false dawn had passed me by. I concluded that because my symptoms had returned, then the answer must lie elsewhere and I went back to doing what I knew - trying to feel different, analysing and fixing.

The irony is that it was not a fluke and I was on to something, but I had made two mistakes. The first one was that I thought I had to feel good all the time and if not then I must be doing something wrong and the second one was that I was using what I learnt as a technique to feel good. So, when I felt terrible and my new attitude did not work, I became frustrated and disillusioned once again. Yet I never gave up on what I learnt that day. Something deep down told me I was on to something here. How I felt for those few days could not have been a fluke, but why did I not stay in that state of peace?

What I eventually realised is that I had suffered a setback that day where all my feelings returned. I actually don't even like the word setback, as it sounds like you have gone backwards when this is not the case. It just means your body is releasing more of what you have suppressed and your mind going through a process of healing from all you have previously put it through.

When I truly understood this, I looked back on that day and recognised my mistake. Feeling good had been great, but having experienced some peace, my body needed another clear-out and my brain needed far more than a few days rest to heal. I honestly did not know that this was a vital part of recovery and that it was a cycle I needed to go through to finally feel peace once again. What I should have done that day is enjoyed the release, as bad as it felt, and seen it as an opportunity to get rid of some more of the anxious and emotional energy stored up within me and welcomed my brain taking the break it needed.

After this realisation I remember going back to allowing once more and feeling great for a few days, then 'WHAM' one of the worst days ever and every cell in my body wanted to fight it off and try to change how I felt. In the midst of it all, it was nearly impossible to see it as a setback. Surely anxiety this strong meant I was worse than ever? But I carried on with my day the best way I could and within two days it was gone and I woke up feeling such peace and clarity. It was the first time in all my suffering where I felt I had gone back to square one and never tried to do anything about it. In the past, these kinds of setbacks would have lasted for weeks as I tried to battle and think my way back to how I previously felt, analysed why I had gone backwards and filled myself with so much self-pity.

This is why in the past, I stayed in a cycle because any previous attempt at a release was fought and suppressed and just topped up with more suffering through my attempts at denying it. My brain could also not take the break it so needed as I would be back overthinking, analysing and fighting once again.

The reason these releases were coming so strong at this particular time was that, for the first time in ten years, I no longer tried to deny or suppress my uncomfortable emotions or anxious feelings. It was the first time I had really opened up and allowed a release to happen, so because of this, the release was quite intense.

The way I started to view setbacks was to recognise that any internal mayhem that occurred was due to my mind and body trying to get back towards balance and return to their natural state. It's a bit like a TV trying to tune itself in. The tuning has to go through a fuzzy period to get back to the perfect picture. When I started to view setbacks in this way, then I actually looked forward to the next release because I knew that a lot of my stored up anxious energy and emotional baggage was leaving me and my brain was taking the break it needed. Sometimes these setbacks would last for a day or two and sometimes they could last up to a week, but the longer, the better, for me as I knew they were vital for my recovery.

At first, it can be like opening up a dam and these releases can come thick and fast. But once you truly understand them and don't go back to your old ways of coping and allow a release to happen, they become far less frequent and don't come with as much force. In my case, they came every few days at first, but towards the end, I totally forgot about them. They were so infrequent and weak that they hardly registered until eventually they never came at all. Everything that I had previously created and suppressed had now pretty much left me and my brain had now recovered from all the mental exhaustion I had previously created.

You may have to go through many cycles of release depending on how long you have suffered and how much you have suppressed. It's just a process of releasing all those trapped emotions, be it anxiety or anything else you have refused to face. I went through many releases, but without fail, they always passed, they always do. When you feel some peace, it's just the end of another release. People who take longer to come out of a setback are the ones who continually fight them and go back to suppressing how they feel. So, call it a process, a setback or a release; it doesn't matter what you call it as long as you know it's a vital part of recovery.

Anxiety is purely excess energy in your body created through a prolonged period of stress or worry. When you feel anxiety arise, then the body is trying to free you of this energy. So, your body is doing you a massive favour, it doesn't want this anxious energy within as much as you and why it brings it to the surface. The trouble is that people don't see setbacks as a release. They see them as a return of their symptoms and so start fighting, worrying and analysing all over again, creating more of what their body is trying to get rid of while continuing to exhaust themselves mentally. That was my mistake that day. I had a real chance to progress, but because I was not educated enough and did not understand that setbacks are a vital part of recovery, I blew it.

So now that you know what a true setback is and how vital they are to your recovery allow each release to happen instead of fearing and denying them like you may have done previously. Begin to observe them, instead of fearing them. See if you can look upon them as nothing more than your body trying to release some fearful, anxious energy or some other trapped emotions. This energy can also take the form of sadness, insecurity or irritability. Whatever is coming up, just allow it to release itself without identifying with it. By this, I mean that if you feel some fearful energy arise, don't hook on to it and believe there is anything outside of you to fear. If you experience some deep sadness coming up, don't identify with this energy and think your life is suddenly awful. Don't take this energy to be who you are. Don't allow it to become you; just see it as old suppressed stuff coming up to be released.

A lot of sufferers only have to deal with the release of anxious/fearful energy, but for some, setbacks can be mental too. We can put the mind through so much and, as previously stated, this can lead to it becoming exhausted. When we finally surrender and so cease worrying, analysing and overthinking, then we will still feel the effects of an exhausted mind, as it still has to go through a process of healing. Even during this process, one day, it may feel fresh and clear and on another, it may feel completely grotty. I also had to go through this back and forth process as my mind healed from what I had previously put it through. One day I would feel great and then the next I could feel immense mental discomfort. Again, I just allowed myself to go through this process of healing without trying to fight, obsess or worry about it (which is what created the problem in the first place). I allowed the mental discomfort to be present and in time, with this new attitude, my mind began to heal itself. I then began to experience real periods of clarity and less discomfort until one day, my mind regained its sense of calm and my mental health returned.

Someone on my Facebook page recently asked a question about setbacks which I have printed below, followed by a member's response:

Original Question: This 'transitional phase' between being anxious and being normal has been hovering over me for a while now and I simply accept it as a beneficial part of recovery. Does this phase last forever?

Members Reply: I've been like that for a while now and I get days/weeks of feeling completely normal then I'll randomly feel weird again. This will last for a couple of days and then I feel fine again. It just goes back and forth for a while until it finally passes. It is normal and fine, so don't worry; it's all part of the healing process.

That is precisely the attitude they both need

Chapter 13

Other People's Stories of Recovery

Recently I asked people on my blog and Facebook page to send in their own stories of recovery. I wanted to add these as I believe they give people great hope and insight into what is needed to recover. I have also been told that it was one of the chapters in the first book that others enjoyed reading the most.

Each one published is from a genuine person and is a true story of their recovery. The response I received to asking people to share their story was overwhelming and I have been unable to publish them all, but here are the ones I thought would be the most helpful and inspiring.

Tim's Story

Through a process of not handling stress very well over a period of time, I fell into one of the darkest days I have ever experienced. Years upon years of refusing to graciously accept little stressors in my life as a given and attempting to make my environment suit me as opposed to me conforming to my environment lead to a level of despair that I didn't even think was possible.

On February 13th of 2013, I woke up at 3:30 in the morning. My mind was just buzzing with activity. There was no thought, in particular, that was bothering me, but every thought that crossed my mind early that morning was charged with such an intensely negative 'feel' to it. I had no clue what was wrong and I couldn't get back to sleep.

The following night when I was attempting to go to sleep, an odd thing occurred, one that had never happened before:

every time I started drifting off, I would immediately find myself awake and alert. This cycle played out the entire night. It was then I knew something was wrong.

During the day my mind started latching on to the thought "Will you be able to sleep tonight?" Over the following days, and restless nights, that thought became charged with so much negative emotion that a flood of fear, doubt and despair would overtake me. I was in a full fit of panic, exhausted, sweating profusely and stomach churning, while my mind plummeted to new depths of despair.

There were other symptoms aside from an inability to sleep (constantly alert, intrusive thoughts, very jumpy, uncomfortable in social settings, no appetite, racing heart) but the sleep issue struck me to my core.

In a matter of a few days, the depression set in. I now felt detached from everything in my life. My wife and I had a son six months earlier, but it seemed that nothing could prevent my stay in total despair and hopelessness. Suicide and thoughts of death were never too far from my mind. I knew it was as bad as it could get when I found myself driving down the road and pleading with God to allow some accident to happen so that I could leave this life behind me and simply cease to exist.

It's one thing to have your future stained with despair, but all of my thoughts from my past, my old calm and peaceful thoughts were now also stained. Those once joyful thoughts and memories now were sources of torment. I felt alien in my own life; a husk of my former self, irreparably broken.

I went to see my primary care physician, a psychologist and a psychiatrist. I'll at least give credit to my primary care physician for not trying to venture any solution that would only leave me further confused and hopeless. The same can't be said for the psychologist and psychiatrist I saw. The phrase 'wildly incompetent' comes to mind when I think of my interactions with them. One was having me plumb the depths of my childhood for an answer. I love my dad, but for reasons beyond my understanding, the psychologist was helping me to conjure up some anger towards him. Were there really some failings on my dad's part that accounted for all of this. I would ask, "Why now? I'm 36 years old. Why would this all come out now?" His justification for the method was as confusing as the method itself.

He had me also see a psychiatrist. Never was a prescription too far from her hand. In a two-month period of seeing her, she had me on: Ambien cr, Lunesta, Trazadone, Lexapro, and Clonopin.

I no longer even recognised myself. My mind was flooded with fear, doubt, and despair while my body was flooded with pharmaceuticals, I didn't even know existed. On my last appointment with her, she prescribed me Rozerem. I drove home, walked in the house, looked at the prescription, ripped it up and decided I'd rather die than take another pill or see her or the psychologist again.

Very shortly after this, a friend who was also struggling suggested I read a book called *At Last a Life* by Paul David. I had read so many books already and wasn't that keen to trawl through another one, but I decided to give it a shot. I wasn't even reading it properly because I thought it couldn't do anything. But it wasn't long until my mind became enveloped by the book. It just made sense to me. The advice was absurdly simple; certainly simpler than delving into my past with no technique to master or any pill to take.

I started taking Paul's advice as soon as I was done reading the book. I just started living my life again. Off of my shoulders came the weight of trying to work it all out in my head. "Give it the space it wants and move on with your life", Paul advised. There were some immediate but slight improvements. But it wasn't long until that horrid doubt started filling my mind: "Paul really didn't talk about my issue as much as I think he should have. Maybe he wasn't writing this book for someone like me. Maybe I'm broken in a way that is different than himself".

Paul very, very wisely states in his book that he wasn't going to unweave all of the possible symptoms and address them individually. This didn't make sense to me at the time, but eventually, it became profoundly wise. The fear and doubt for each individual can be made to manifest in so many different ways, but even for one person his or her fear and doubt will expand, shift, and contort in ways that can leave a person befuddled. This is one reason why it doesn't matter to even start addressing individual symptoms and expressions of anxiety.

In the end, the advice is still the same: let it be there and live your life.

It wasn't a steady line assent to recovery for me. There were ups and downs and setbacks that made me think that Paul's approach could never work for someone like me. The despair got so thick at one point that I was certain I was irreparably broken. But then a thought dawned upon me, "Even if you are broken and there is no hope for you recovering your old self.... isn't a life lived larger than anxiety better than a life that only focuses on anxiety?" And then I understood what Paul was saying. Before I was giving anxiety the space it needed as long as it was sure to leave, and quickly at that. I didn't truly let it be there; it was always contingent on the hope that it would just leave me alone for good. I also didn't live my life alongside anxiety; anxiety had become my only focus; my only cause of concern. I now realised why I felt so stuck in my own head, unable to connect with the world around me.

At this point, I shed all hope and focus on recovery. That might sound like a terrible idea. But it wasn't. I was simply going to make my life larger than the dictates of anxiety. I would ignore those dictates of anxiety. Not in the sense of pretending that they weren't there, I was just done taking heed of them. They were more than welcome to yell as loud as they wanted to and yell they did.

Even with no focus on recovery, I would have these moments where my mind felt calm, peaceful and normal! Those moments were fleeting and that was fine. My goal now was nothing more than just living my life with or without anxiety. Slowly the sting of the fear, doubt and despair would lessen. Setbacks would still come, but earlier on, I had realised that it just didn't pay to fight against them, to engage them in an argument. All that ever did was get me stuck further in the mire.

I would go from feeling OK to feeling dreadful at times, but I was fine with this, I was still healing. When the setback lifted, things would just make sense; this from no effort on my part. I started to clearly see what Paul meant when he said we are responsible for creating our own suffering. I wasn't doing anything here to feel better; I was just allowing my mind and body to heal in any way they wished to do so. I had stopped all the doing and this is what had started the healing process.

If one needs a goal, then make that goal simply to live your life. There is no need to engage in the world of anxiety, engage in the world around you.

We all know people who are consistently happy. In moments of self-pity (a tendency, from my experience, that sufferers of anxiety indulge in a bit) we get frustrated at them and possibly convince ourselves that we just had it harder than them. This is a lie. People whose lives are defined by happiness, peacefulness, calmness are not the ones who through cunning or luck avoided all the pitfalls that beset us and lead to our anxiety. They are simply the ones who accept all that comes their way, good or bad. They allowed their lives to be larger than the bad things that happen in it, and that graceful allowance became their habit as it can become your habit as well.

"God bless."

Tim now helps on my blog and gives out some fantastic words of advice. This following piece was written by him for someone on there who was struggling and has so much truth in it.

"Hi Shaun, Dominic said it the best when he said "turn your 'what ifs' into 'so what's'.

Stop caring so much. Like Paul said, allow your body or brain to feel and think whatever they wish. Think of how liberating this is as nothing is off limits now when it comes to thoughts and feelings. Allow everything to come. Think of it like this, it's going to come regardless, right? When has freaking out, searching the net and frantically trying to stop it ever helped?

So, open your arms up and embrace all it has to offer. I would have fears and doubts (doubts of ever recovering) so thick that I could feel them crushing me down. Any interest I had in life or things that used to provide enjoyment would be quickly snubbed out by this fear and double, like trying to light a candle in a gale. It was only when, following Paul's advice, I simply let everything come. I allowed myself to be scared, full of fear, full of doubt. I stopped running from those feelings. I stopped trying to rationalise them away (I mean, seriously, has anyone of us ever successfully reasoned away these fears?).

But what did I now do differently? As Dominic said, I turned those 'what ifs' into 'so what's'. I'm personally not a fan of mantras, breathing exercises or any concerted effort to ‘accept’. Again, like Paul said, actively doing things to make this burden lift just doesn’t work. It simply reinforces that this issue is actually a pretty big deal. But that’s not to say that I never had to remind myself. Sometimes I’d tell myself, “it’s okay Tim, it’s fine to feel this way” or “So what? Let it be there. I’m still going to live my life the way I want to.”

These are different to mantras. I’m not endlessly repeating it over and over. I’m not saying it to make those bad feelings and thoughts lift, like so many who use mantras do. I’m simply reminding myself that it’s okay; that anything that happens to my mind or body is okay.

But remember, you still need to get out there and live your life. It’s one thing to say “okay, I’m going to be at peace with this burden”, but to say that and to come back to this blog on a daily basis is simply doing it the wrong way. Come back if you really need to, but if you find it becoming more habitual, then stop.

Remember, this approach is completely liberating. No thought or feeling is off-limits. You are now letting down your guard. Let it all wash over you. Be at peace with the lack of peace in your life, then, in time, you will find true peace.

God Bless

I think you can see there in Tim’s story that recovery is not the giant of a struggle that people believe it to be. It did not entail years of counselling, techniques and mantras or any attempt at trying to get rid of something. When we give up the struggle, great things can happen. Trust me it is the struggle that hurts you so much. I really cannot emphasise this enough.

I got to a stage where I did not particularly like the way I felt, but I no longer struggled, feared or concerned myself with it. Because of this my suffering was greatly reduced and didn’t last anywhere near as long, as I was no longer feeding more worry and concern into my brain. I had cut off a major fuel supply for anxiety and this is what Tim did by allowing himself to feel the way he did, he couldn't deny these emotions, but he certainly had the power not to struggle, worry or concern himself with them.

When that fuel is cut off and you no longer recreate your suffering through more worry and concern, then the mind and body can begin to heal. As now there is no longer a constant stream of fear, worry and concern creating more suffering and keeping you stuck in a loop. I really hope people can see the truth in this and not constantly chase their own tail searching for something to eliminate anxiety or chase their feelings away, as it truly does not work that way.

I will finish with the following statement sent to me by someone who has recovered.

Two people are sent to prison for the same amount of time. One guy is in his cell each night crying with self-pity; one moment banging on the cell walls and the next running through scenarios in his mind of how he can get out. Due to this, he feels terrible and constantly exhausts himself as he refuses to accept his current plight.

The other guy accepts his fate, sits on his bed, takes out a book and starts to read a little before lights out.

Be the other guy.

Rochelle's Story

I just wanted to start out by saying that your book saved my life. I cannot thank you enough for all of the information. I suffered from anxiety and severe depression after the birth of my son on July 7, 2014. I came home the following day with my baby and that night suffered from what I know now was a panic attack and thus my anxiety began. I had every symptom you mention in your book and no answers; I really had no idea what was going on. I thought I'd had a heart attack or something else horrible was happening to me. I ended up in the emergency room and after 5 hours of strenuous tests, I was told that I was okay, which left me utterly bewildered. I then went home and began thinking what could be wrong with me? What had happened to me? And when I initially felt it happening again because I feared another episode, I thought for sure I had postpartum psychosis or some other type of postpartum problem.

I visited doctor after doctor, with no answers. They all just looked at me and wondered why I was so agitated and kept trying to force pills that did not help. I was pushed from therapist to psychiatrist to finally a therapist that did help in some way towards my recovery.

I stayed away from my son at this time and I could not even be around him as I had such disturbing thoughts that I might hurt him or myself. These thoughts seemed irrational but real at the same time. So, I was back into the emergency room because I thought for sure something was terribly wrong. Again, they told me nothing was wrong and I was sent home to try and get better. It was at this point I slowly began to slip into depression. I stopped caring about what I looked like; I stopped eating, stopped sleeping and all because my brain would not stop searching for the answer to this new-found problem.

I tried to explain what I was going through to my husband, but he had no idea; nobody understood. I felt so alone, trying to fight my way out of this hell. I figured I would end up in some institution, never to see my family again. But I began to research what this could be and stumbled upon your site online, and then ordered your book.

When I first went to read it, I suffered from what I can only describe as severe depersonalisation. My anxiety was so bad I could hardly read the book. But I started to read and finally I had found the answers to all the questions that my mind was seeking. It all began to make sense. I basically just gave up the fight. It was very difficult to do, but I did it. I had many, many bad days thinking I will be stuck in this hell forever, but I just stayed with the advice and things began to change.

I began to have moments of quiet in my mind. The tools in your book really started to help and I was so relieved. It was so good and was such a weight off my mind to no longer be searching and fighting. It was such a relief to hear through your words that I wasn't going crazy and was not about to be carted off anywhere. Yes, there were still many days where I wanted to give up, thinking I would never smile again, never be able to take care of my children or love my husband. But then I realised that the anxiety was there to help me. It was a warning system that things had gone too far and I had overdone things. It really was a friend that was asking me to stop the worry and the stress.

I had to read your book many times to let the information really sink in, but slowly, very slowly, my mind began to reverse these habits I had started and though I don't feel I'm 100% recovered, I know that full recovery is just around the corner as I am so much better. I can now do all of the things I could do before, including taking care of my son. I made myself smile on the days where it was impossible and never gave up. I realise now how important life really is and how important friends and family are.

Though I can say I hope I never reach that place again, I know that I can get through it and because of it, I am a better person. I realise now how important your health is. You really just need to get on with your life and take the anxiety with you, and man is it sometimes the hardest thing to do, because all my anxiety wanted me to do was stay in bed. But I refused to let my emotions take charge; I started to see them as just harmless thoughts and emotions and due to this, they lost so much power. Looking back that makes so much sense as when I was petrified of the way I felt and thought, then, of course, I was adding more anxiety, stress and worry and this was the reason I felt so terrible.

To others that are suffering from anxiety, you will get through it. And believe me, I was one of those who thought, "Yeah right, I'm going to be like this forever; my life is over". But just let go of the fight, just let your body heal itself and never give up. There is so much to live for.

Thank you so much again Paul for all of the information you provided me, without it I really don't know where I would be now. I really thought I wouldn't make it out of that hell and I was ready to give up. But I never did and I thank God every day for that decision. I sincerely hope my story helps provide hope to someone.

I really cannot thank you enough, Paul, you gave me my life back.

Scotty's Story

I'd wanted to live in America ever since I was a little kid. I think it was a case of watching too much 'Saved by The Bell' leading me to develop a desire to either be Zack Morris or to be with Kelly Kapowski – I'm not sure which. Anyway, at the age of 29, I had that opportunity and so in the summer of 2013, I headed out on a five-year visa to Washington DC. I'd been working for a small and specialised professional services firm who wanted me to help build out the office over there and I have to say I was very excited. I turned down a great job in London where I was living at the time with another firm and couldn't wait to get started. Things, however, didn't quite work out the way I'd planned.

Within two weeks of moving over there, the partner I was working with quit and I ended up taking on a large proportion of his work. This meant I was then working 70-80 hour weeks, including Saturday and Sunday. Early the next year my girlfriend, with whom I had agreed to go long distance, dumped me and the company decided to close the DC office and move me to New York. This would mean another relocation and home move. I hadn't made any friends due to my work commitments and had started having funny turns that I didn't understand – shortness of breath, racing heart etc. I shrugged these off, however, and thought nothing of them. It wasn't long though before an incident that was the straw that broke the camel's back came along.

Dentistry in the UK is a medical service, at least on the NHS. In the US it's big business. This is a fact I was naively unaware of in early 2014. To cut a long story short, I had a lot of work done – which future dentists told me I didn't need – and it made a mess of my mouth. I couldn't open it more than a quarter inch, I had migraines essentially the entire waking day as well as shooting pains down my neck and into my back. Sensitive teeth to the point where I could only eat lukewarm soup through a straw and the tightening of my facial muscles to the point it felt as though I'd had a facelift.

Adding this to the stress working in a high-pressure, results-driven environment on the other side of the world with no support network, I essentially crumbled. When the dentist told me things might never get better, I went back to work and had my first panic attack at my desk. I then made every mistake in the book. I fought it, wrestled with it, tried to drive it away, ran around looking for an answer and did everything possible to add fuel to the fire. At the same time, I continued to work, and while living a normal life is essential to recovery, neither the environment I was in nor my current mindset were conducive to success! Before too long, I had a full-on nervous breakdown and went on to experience a litany of physical and mental symptoms over the coming nine months. Even after another dentist helped correct the issues with my teeth, these only got worse.

So few people knew how bad I was. Here is a list of those I can remember – intrusive and disturbing thoughts, constant inexplicable heightened levels of fear, inability to quiet my mind, constant worry, self-pity, self-loathing, depression, shaking, adrenaline rushes, restless legs, chest pain, heart racing, stabbing feeling in the stomach, sweating, pins and needles, headaches, vomiting, loss of appetite, increased appetite, digestive system shutdown, crying for no reason, overly emotional responses to trivial matters, dry retching, tight throat, overproduction of mucus, shortness of breath, insomnia all the way through to depersonalisation and derealisation. Each symptom was heightened by between five and ten panic attacks a day. It wasn't ideal.

Then, after about six weeks of denying there was anything wrong, I decided to do something about it. I first met a psychiatrist who came highly recommended. He diagnosed me with severe generalised anxiety and panic attacks and tried to put me on anti-depressants within ten minutes of walking through his door. He told me I would probably need to be on these for the rest of my life. I worked with him for six weeks but didn't take the pills. In the interests of full disclosure, he did prescribe some tranquiliser type medication for the panic attacks and between May 2014 and July 2014, I probably took somewhere between 15 and 20 of these.

It was about this time that I read Paul David's first book, *At Last a Life*. It made some sense to me, but to be honest, it wasn't what I wanted to hear. It wasn't a quick fix. So, I ignored it and instead, over the next three months, I tried a lot of different things to get better. These included, but were not limited to, a therapist who told me to try press-ups, hypnotherapy, relaxation retreats, various methods, diet change, vitamins, minerals and a whole bunch of other stuff. Little changed and I was still just as bad, if not growing a little more hopeless.

Somewhere in amongst all this, I had stopped working and moved back to the UK. The flight home was interesting, to say the least. It was four months in and I was at my wits' end when I came across a psychologist who specialised in anxiety. A lot, though not all, of what he taught was similar to what Paul teaches. He helped a lot in putting me on the right path and I went as far as I could with him. To truly get better, however, I knew I had to accept things and move through the feelings on my own. I then went back and re-read *At Last a Life* and decided to apply Paul's teachings.

Within days some of my symptoms lessened and within weeks, I had an hour or so of clarity. A month or so later it was a couple of days, then weeks on end. I've had four major setbacks, the last of which was the week between Christmas and New Year 2014. I still have the very odd twinge, but now it's gone within minutes if not seconds. These are less and less frequent and, to be honest, I can't remember the last one.

I just began to accept how I was feeling rather than constantly fight against it. I got back out there and lived my life, despite feeling like I was dying much of the time. I reclaimed my independence, moving out of a friend's spare room and back into my own flat, taking responsibility for myself. I have gone back to work and started my own business. I have been on holidays abroad and I have built relationships with new people. I have gone towards what frightened me, and come out the other side. I now genuinely love life again. The only task I have ahead of me is to shed some weight after all of the comfort eating!

There were other things that helped, like a better diet and more exercise, but acceptance and the teachings that Paul espouses were the real things that led me to a successful recovery - acceptance, non-avoidance and independence. In my opinion and experience, if you want to move through anxiety, then these are the principles you have to adopt.

Catherine's Story

Anxiety first hit me last year off the back of a new high responsibility job and a difficult break-up. Stress had crept in over the year and I was getting myself more and more wound up until bam, the first panic attack happened. I remember it like it was yesterday. Fear set in from that very moment. *What is happening to my mind? Why? How can I make sure this doesn't happen again?* I spent pretty much an entire weekend shaking, severely anxious, pain in my chest and throat. I rushed to A&E, thinking I had heart problems only to be told to go home and relax. It was from then on that problems just grew and grew – the fear of those feelings coming back encompassed me and anxiety had become my anxiety.

I developed severe GAD to the point where my entire day was spent anxious and all I did was feed the condition with more worries. I lost my appetite, I had constant pain in my throat, I became depressed, I didn't think anyone understood (they didn't really) so I felt totally isolated. The GP referred me to a course of CBT – all I said during my sessions was "Why is this happening to me?" and attempting to find the positive equivalent to that thought which just added stress to my mind. I quit my job, which I loved. I had a month off but spent it feeling anxious and even more depressed for not having a job anymore. Crying was a momentary relief. Knowing that anxiety would be back once the crying ended was hell. It was an endless loop. I took on a different job, no change, and I quit six weeks later. By my third job, I was at rock bottom, so unwell and resigned within two months completely in despair. I rented out my room and went home to my parents' house again.

When I found Paul's website and book, things started to change. It was in no way an immediate fix, but something about his approach stuck with me and although I veered away from it several times, it really was the only thing that started to instigate change. Let it happen. It seemed so simple. Of course, just let it happen. Not as easy as it sounds. But wow, has it been worth it. I have been through some of the worst days of my life since I started putting Paul's advice into practice and have been lower than I've ever been. And some days I felt it was impossible and lost all faith. *What if recovery doesn't really exist? What if people just say you recover, but you don't really?* But the next day would come around and I'd go again and if I experienced even a few seconds of relief in that day, a light in my mind would come on and a smidgen of hope would raise its head.

When I started to see bigger and more lasting improvements, I then called my old boss up from the job I loved. He asked very few questions and let me come back to work. I am eternally grateful to him for this. Once I started recovering, I saw how much I had thrown away unnecessarily. Panic attacks came, doubt came, depression came and somehow, I just kept getting through it and started to realise that there were moments during the day where I felt OK, even if just for five minutes. I stopped reaching out to so many people whenever I panicked and let it play itself out by myself a bit more. I'd contact friends or family to say 'I just let a panic attack happen' instead of 'Help me, I'm panicking', which started to empower me ever so slightly. Only I knew what my mind was doing, and I knew that this approach was changing something.

There were moments where my mind seemed so clear that I could touch the healthy me. There was no longer any black cloud or terrifying feeling encompassing me and I'd feel better than I ever felt. Then the next day, I'd be back down again, so low and fearful that I could barely remember the good moment the day before. I realised that I was learning and improving when, in one of my darker days, I called a counsellor thinking *I cannot live with this anymore! This is ridiculous*! and she started talking to me about breathing techniques, medication and an anxiety app. I just thought, *No, she doesn't get it at all. She hasn't been through it. I know more than this woman about this.* So, I just said "No thank you" and hung up. Everything I needed to make myself feel better was within me and I knew this now more than ever.

I started doing everything socially that I did before and took the hellish feelings with me, however bad it got, letting it be there and continuing with life. I didn't analyse how tomorrow was going to go. I just went with; however I was feeling in the moment. Slowly, I was able to enjoy things again, laugh and enjoy sport and social occasions. I'm not saying anxiety left me completely at first. I'm saying I enjoyed these things regardless and started to care about anxiety less. I then started talking about it more to those closest to me, started a blog to share Paul's incredible advice and one day a few weeks back I had an entire day where I felt anxiety free - all day. It was incredible. It just crept up on me.

It was a day like no other I have experienced to date in my life. I had stopped aiming for any kind of freedom and yet here it was, just like that. I felt so happy. The next day I had the physical stuff again but knowing that that day had existed just drove me to continue.

I've now realised that anxiety is a very convincing trick. It's totally empty of point or necessity. It is the attempt to solve something that was never there in the first place. I have spent so much time and energy trying to figure things out, solve problems, find the right way of doing things, how to fix myself, what I can do better, when in fact there is absolutely nothing to figure out or fix; nothing at all. I'm attempting to resolve a problem which doesn't exist! No wonder I've had panic after panic! As soon as I realised that I just needed to let the problem (that doesn't exist) go, I felt better. Is that not the main aim? When you get into the habit of worrying, you very easily slip into *'But there is something to worry about. What is it today?'* because somehow it makes us feel like we are controlling things or keeping ourselves safe. Actually no, you're not controlling anything; you're just making yourself feel like crap.

I can still have the odd wave of anxiety and unease, but my mindset has changed so much now that I almost couldn't care less if this is as good as it gets (which I know it is not). Because it doesn't stop me doing a thing or having fun and it just does not bother me at all anymore. I know it's all one big trick and I keep on welcoming it like a little buddy. I clearly see now that there is nothing you can do to change the natural journey of your emotions, especially when you are healing. There's nothing you can do but allow them and feel them all, be they good or bad. It's a tough journey, but I know it's the way to go.

Anxiety has made my life fuller as I now see every day for the gift that it truly is. I am much less swayed by anyone else's opinion now and am so much more self-assured and confident in myself. I appreciate everything, absolutely everything. Anxiety is the single, most positive thing that has ever happened to me. It taught me how to live and perceive things differently, it took me by the end and taught me to no longer worry and stress about minor things and to appreciate life and others far more. I am so excited about life now and this new understanding I have of myself. I am eternally grateful to Paul; I owe him everything for sharing his story.

Thank you is not enough, Paul.

Alyssa's Story

When we are born into this world, those before us are likely to assume that we will live what they would call a typical life. You know, like achieving life's typical milestones. More than likely you will experience your first day of kindergarten, somehow earn your driver's license, graduate from high school and maybe college, dance with your dad at your wedding, cry tears of joy with your mom after having your first baby. Then send your kids off to college, and grow old with your spouse, all the while enjoying every minute of it.

Although every individual lives with the expectation that all of these things will happen to them just like everyone else, for some it is either suddenly stripped from their future or diluted with doom, and if this occurs, you can either roll with the punches and just live your life or have these things literally eat you alive.

For me, my world was flipped upside down the day my mom passed away when I was nineteen (we didn't even know she had cancer). One day my biggest dilemma was picking a country on which to do my Spanish project and the next was choosing which coffin my mom would have liked. There was no long battle with chemo, which I suppose I'm thankful for, but the path she had chosen was still laden with unimaginable suffering for us all.

I always wondered what it would be like to lose someone you truly believe you can't live without - a part of me even yearned to experience it one day just to see what would happen or how I would handle it. Would it be like the movies? Would it be like one of Shakespeare's tragedies? I always thought that these actors and characters were exaggerating just to earn an Oscar or make a story more memorable (it's just fiction, after all), but it wasn't until I experienced loss first-hand that I finally realised that all these gut-wrenching emotions weren't just added for flare. No, these emotions were real.

My sister and I were waiting amidst vases of flowers we had just bought for our mom in her new room at the hospital when my dad told us that she had passed away in the elevator. Without even thinking, I dropped whatever was in my hands and shoved myself in the nearest corner, bawling my eyes out. I had never cried like that before; my body just couldn't stop shaking as I fought to see through my mascara-stained glasses. I had completely forgotten about the host of relatives that were gently stroking my hair from behind for who knows how long.

I sometimes wonder what they were thinking in a time like that because from the outside they looked like they still had control of their sanity. I hardly remember the week leading up to her funeral, but somewhere in there, I managed to type up her eulogy and buy a new black dress (she was never fond of the one that I usually wore). The funeral itself really wasn't that bad surprisingly, that is, until the slideshow started. But even just days after the funeral, I genuinely thought I was okay—not great, mind you, but okay. It wasn't until much later that I realised how affected I was.

It happened a little over a month after my mom's death. I was sitting in our local movie theatre, watching the world's latest take on the story of Noah with my family when it hit me. In an instant, my heart was racing at what felt like a hundred miles an hour. My lungs were fighting to expand against what felt like a tightly cinched corset around my chest. My hands shook as if I kept touching a hot skillet over and over, my senses never learning to refrain from the heat. My eyes could no longer focus on the massive screen directly ahead of me. The urge to pass out overtook my entire body. I desperately tried to get more comfortable in my seat and nibbled on popcorn in a poor attempt to get a hold of myself, but all I really managed to do was keep myself distracted until the end of the film (thankfully we had already gone through most of it). Immediately afterwards, I told my sister that I was about to pass out and needed to go home, thinking I just needed to get a little something to eat and rest for the night. After my dad drove us home, I crawled into bed and morphed myself into the tightest little ball I could muster, praying that I would eventually find peace in sleep.

It wasn't, but a few days after when the struggle to breathe proved too much to cope with, it had now gotten to the point where each breath felt like my last. I was hyperventilating in a desperate attempt to get more oxygen. Although it was the last place they wanted to return to, my dad and my little sister took one look at me and didn't think twice about rushing me to the ER. There, nurses quickly tethered me to various beeping instruments via wires and stickers after taking a quick x-ray of my chest.

As we were waiting for the results of my chest x-ray, I just *knew* that they would find something wrong. Fluid in my lungs, a tumour, a blood clot, anything that would explain why my body acted like it was fighting for its life. But when the doctor came back with the results, all he had to show us was the ghostly grey imaging of a perfectly sound heart guarded by a set of healthy larger-than-average lungs. I remember thinking that this just couldn't be right, that I must be looking at someone else's x-ray instead of my own. But no, this scan was mine. I could easily read HIGGINS, ALYSSA M. typed in bold white font along the bottom of the image.

What the doctor did next was something that I would have never guessed in a million years: he diagnosed me with severe anxiety. I just lay there in disbelief as the words that shot at me like daggers leisurely rolled off his tongue (apparently my father had mentioned to the doctor while I was in for my x-ray that my mom had just recently passed). Once I got my bearings back, I asked him if more imaging could be done to make sure, but he told me that it was too late in the night and that they would have to call others in from home that were specifically certified for those screenings (I could tell he was writing me off). Eventually, it got to the point where he insisted that nothing was wrong with me and sent me home with nothing more than a doctor's note and a prescription for some anxiety medication that I would never consider taking. Going home that night felt like such a defeat. I had stopped hyperventilating, but I didn't feel any better. All I felt like now was like a crazy person, but far worse - a crazy person without the slightest hope.

The next few months consisted of many different ups and downs (mostly downs, to be honest). I had managed to finish off my classes for that semester, but the following summer was one that I would like to forget. Sure, I went swimming with my cousins frequently and even took a much-needed family vacation to Atlanta, but during these times, I still felt like my body could break down on itself at any given moment. At any time, I could be the bedbound nut-job I once was when I had just returned from the ER.

Anxiety has a way of swinging you back and forth like some plaything. Once it tires of you, it will seem like it has lost interest in you for a while, but it always seems to have a way of charging uninvited through your door again. I cried and prayed continuously whenever anxiety physically wrecked my body and once the symptoms seemed to be at bay, I would soak up the opportunity and pretend to live normally for as long as I could until my body decided to turn on me once again. I had hoped that my next semester at college would keep my mind off of how bad I felt inside, but this was not to be. I was able to pretend for a while and put on a happy face during class or afterwards with peers, but the month before finals I had once again become a slave to my fears.

I was once again housebound. The thought of returning to school was almost unbearable; I couldn't even make a trip to the grocery store without bursting into tears. I was so uncoordinated that I felt like I could pass out at any given moment. My mind whirled like a top; always analysing, always questioning. Why me? What do these symptoms mean? Am I going to die? When will this nightmare end? I spent most of my time either crying or Googling my new latest symptom (neither of which did absolutely anything for me but put even more stress on my already exhausted body).

However, while surfing the web, I had stumbled upon a particular website that wasn't at all like other anxiety forums that seemed to only terrify me more. This one was entitled "Anxietynomore" and was run by an ex-anxiety sufferer by the name of Paul David. He too had dealt with severe anxiety, for ten years in fact, and had wandered helplessly down the road of countless prescriptions and doctor's appointments until he finally had the realisation that he alone had the ability to regain his old life back.

For the first time, I felt hope as I combed over the entire website with a fine-toothed comb, leaving no link unread. There was no talk of some magic pill or miracle cure, which was quite refreshing after the countless gimmicks I had encountered that had promised such things (you would be surprised of some of the things you find on the Internet), but of how to conquer anxiety ON YOUR OWN. Without even having a chance to think about it, I ordered Paul's book, which has undoubtedly become my biggest step towards freedom thus far.

I now have a whole new mentality when it comes to my anxiety. I no longer fuel it further with fear, but face it head-on with what I can only call a "so what" attitude. Instead of stressing my body out even more with constant worry like I once did, I now allow my mind and body to do as they wish without obstruction. Sure, it may not be the most comfortable thing in the world, but I have finally realised that it is in no way life-threatening; it's all a trick. Everyone deals with bouts of adrenaline when they feel scared or anxious; my body just over exaggerates a bit due to the constant worry that has plagued my mind for so long. My anxiety is no longer being fed with fear and panic but is slowly being starved by just not caring and living my life and for the very first time since I first struggled with anxiety, my mind is also getting the break it so desperately needs. Looking back, I can't believe what I put it through, the worry, the stress, fear, questions, my poor brain just couldn't handle it all and broke down, it is now just a question of no longer putting it through that and allowing it to heal.

I now know that one day I will once again be the person that I once was, the difference in me from the person who first encountered anxiety is unrecognisable.

I truly hope my story helps people in some way

Kate's Story

A while ago, my life was going so smoothly that I never for one moment thought I could end up in the hole that I did. I had no inclination that anxiety even existed and if I had, I would not have a clue about how it could take over my life.

My struggles began after I left college and moved away from my family and friends to be with my partner in another town. At first, this adventure was exciting and new; sharing an apartment with the love of my life was everything I dreamed of. I also got a new job and found new friends, and things were looking better than ever. But, like anything in life, the highs don't last forever. Living with someone was nowhere near as exciting as the long-distance relationship we once shared. I also missed my family and old friends. My new friends were great, but they weren't the ones I grew up with. As time passed, I knew that I was really missing home and this started to affect my relationship to the point where we started bickering constantly. The endless fall-outs then led to him staying out and coming home drunk at all hours.

We argued constantly and, the more we argued, the less time we spent together and the more I missed home. It all came to a head one day when he stayed out all night without contact. I stayed up all night wondering where he was and couldn't sleep. It was at this point that everything seemed to hit me and I felt extremely anxious and not myself. I couldn't say exactly what was wrong, but I just felt different; kind of detached and emotionless. I decided that day that enough was enough, told my partner it was over, packed my bags and went home.

The real problems started when I arrived home. My relationship had broken down and I had no job to come back to. Some of my friends had moved on, I was struggling to get my social life back on track and the lack of money certainly didn't help. I just woke up one day and did not want to get out of bed. My thoughts seemed to be racing all over the place and I had no energy or motivation to face the outside world.

When I did venture out, my surroundings seemed different. Everything looked flat, dark and uninviting and I was soon retreating back home to the safety of my bedroom. I would say nothing to my family about the way I felt as I did not want to worry them and I think they just thought that I was feeling down because of the break-up. I kept things to myself as I did not want to worry anyone and, apart from that, I presumed these feelings would be gone soon and I would be back to my old self.

It was only after a few weeks of feeling like this and realising that things were not improving that I went to see my doctor. I could no longer deny anything was wrong and I realised I wasn't just going to wake up and this would be gone. My zest for life had completely diminished, everything now seemed flat and one-dimensional and I still felt constantly anxious. It was as though I was in a constant state of worry even if I had nothing to worry about. But it was the constant racing thoughts that plagued me more than anything; I just wanted some peace from them.

It was hard to begin to tell the doctor what was wrong, as I did not know myself, but after I had explained my symptoms, she finally said, "I think you have anxiety due to all the recent stress that you have gone through". On hearing this, I was instantly relieved that I was not going crazy and how I felt had a name.

The doctor initially offered me some pills that I picked up from my local chemist. I was on my way home, praying that these would be the answer to all my problems, but after taking them, I just felt zoned out. After this, I switched tablets many times before I finally decided that pills were not for me and so, with the help of my doctor, I gradually came off them.

It was after the failed tablets route that I then turned to the internet to try and find out more about anxiety and educate myself on this condition. What I initially found was of little to no help. I was constantly told to do certain techniques that seemed to point towards controlling or suppressing my thoughts and feelings, which certainly never made me feel any better. In between that, I paid a small fortune for a bunch of CD's and, well, let's just say I fell for this once and never went down that road again.

After all this futile searching and finding nothing of any real help, I was basically left alone to my own devices, picking up the odd book and struggling each day to make sense of how I felt. Then one day, I came across Paul's site, bought his book and soaked up what he had to say. Something just instantly clicked, as he was the only one I had so far come across that told me that I need not do anything and that it was this constant search for peace that was keeping me stuck. I don't know if I believed this at first, but something in his words rang true. I wanted to believe it as I always had this desire to do nothing and go back to living my life.

It was only when I read what Paul said: *"feeling better comes from no longer trying to feel better"* that I had one of those lightbulb moments. Something about that sentence made me feel excited; it made real sense to me, as trying to feel better was so exhausting. I just had this momentary realisation that I was the one doing this to myself. I then went downstairs, made a sandwich and looked at my father reading his paper without a care in the world and, once again, something clicked. I thought to myself *"Look, my dad is not putting himself through what I am each day and he is fine. What if trying to feel better had been the cause and not the cure, just like Paul said?"*

Before I suffered from anxiety, I just lived out my life without the need to figure it all out. I was not worrying about anything internally 24/7. I now realised what Paul was saying and that it was not the initial anxiety I felt when I first got home that was the problem, it was the constant need to fix it and work it out that had brought me to this stage. If I had just allowed that initial anxiety to release itself without questioning it, worrying about it and fighting it, then I would have never ended up as I am now. All that did was to create another bunch of symptoms to question, worry and stress about. When I saw this, I just sat at the end of my bed and cried. I could now finally see some light at the end of the tunnel after going down so many blind alleys.

I then went back and re-read all the things Paul had to say and then everything just clicked. It was like reading a different book. I did not need a technique to follow or implement; he wasn't asking me to do anything. This was such a relief as I was tired of looking for cures and answers, tired of using techniques and sayings just to get through the day, tired of battling against my thoughts/feelings and tired of analysing. Yet, previously, I thought it was what I had to do to survive each day. I never for one moment, thought I could just stop doing all of this.

Even after I saw all this, things were quite shaky for a while and I had some real up and down phases. But I learnt to just ride these periods out without any resistance and refused to fall back into the old habits of freaking out, analysing or trying to fix anything. I understood that this was a process I had to go through. It had taken me plenty of time to reach this current state and so it made sense that it would take a while before I felt like my old self again. How I felt now was perfectly normal and I would treat it as such.

The story above was me two years ago and now I can say that I am fully recovered. I have a new partner, a new job and life is great once again. I know that without Paul's advice, I would still be where I was. All I can say to anyone who suffers from anxiety is to let go of that battle with yourself as there truly is nothing to work out and certainly nothing to fix. Just let it all play out as it does. Give your mind and body space to heal without your constant attempts at manipulation, and peace will find you. As Paul says, the real you is always there, just like the sun behind a dark cloud. The sun is you, untouchable by anything anxiety can bring along.

I hope my story gives help and inspiration to anyone who reads it.

Chapter 14

Q & A Section

Below are a small number of questions I have been asked over the years. I decided to publish the ones that come up often and felt would be the most helpful to others.

Question: *Paul, you talk about allowing, accepting and being at peace with how you feel. Can you elaborate please as I still get confused with exactly what this concept means?*

Someone said to me last week 'Paul I have been allowing myself to feel how I do, yet I still felt bad all last week. Any advice as to what I am doing wrong?'

Well, there are many things wrong with this statement. Firstly, he is as far as he could be from allowing his experience, as he is still complaining about it. So, he is not allowing anything; if he were, then it wouldn't have mattered to him how he felt. Secondly, he falsely thinks he should feel good all the time and, lastly, he has attempted to use my words as a technique to rid himself of his feelings, not allow.

Let's get past the myth that any of my words are to be used to get rid of something or to make you feel good. They aren't; in fact, quite the opposite. By that, I mean that it's OK not to feel OK. Don't waste time and energy trying to change your experience, don't spend hours analysing it and don't spend hours worrying about it, otherwise, you will keep yourself in a loop of suffering.

It is all about no longer trying to change your experience and just allowing it to be as it is without trying to control or manipulate it. It is just walking away from the battle, getting on with your life and letting things unfold as they do, uncomfortable or not. The person above has not done this; if he had, then he would not have cared if he felt good or bad last week.

You have to understand that you have no control over how you feel, if you could change it then you would have succeeded by now. Trying to manipulate your current state just recreates the suffering you are trying to escape from. When this is seen clearly then a surrender happens automatically,

The best way I can explain this is to say: Imagine you had a big bowl of water and you shook it from side to side and the water started sloshing around. What would be the best way to get the water to settle? It would be to leave it alone. You can't force it to settle. Any attempt will just unsettle it further and then, of course, it never settles. So, the paradox is, the more you try to make it settle, the more unsettled it becomes and this is true when we start to battle with our mind and emotional state.

The more you try to manage your inner experience then the more uncomfortable and unsettled you become. It took me a long time to realise that the best way to control my experience was to give up all control of it, but when I did, finally things began to improve.

Question: *I love what you write and it has helped me a lot, but although I would not call it depression, I still feel down quite a lot and end up turning to other things like food to feel better. Do you have anything to help with feeling down?*

There is absolutely nothing wrong with feeling down. Welcome to being human; it's all part of our make-up. We live in a world where we are told happiness is a must and feeling low is bad and why we see so many new buzzwords and life coaches popping up. Imagine someone saying to you: 'Right, your life aim is to be always happy.' My reply would be 'Huh, can't I just feel both happy and sad like everyone else? That would be so much easier. I'm not wasting time and energy trying to feel a certain way all the time; that would be impossible'. It is like saying that it must always be sunny out and never rain. Part of the human experience is that our moods go up and down. Even the most enlightened person on the planet will still have times when they feel down.

If you allow any sadness to arrive without trying to fight it, without trying to escape it and without putting a story around it, then you are doing nothing wrong and it will pass when it is ready.

Anxiety sufferers going through a process of recovery can feel quite drained and flat, so don't worry if you feel lower than normal at this present time. It's only when you put a label on it as bad or wrong and then start trying to change how you feel, that it becomes a problem.

The main reason people look to escape a low mood is because they are under the false impression that we must always feel good. People spend their whole life seeking pleasure and avoiding pain. This is why so many people turn to food, drugs, alcohol and other things like excessive shopping. All of which may help temporarily, but in the long run, make things worse, leading to them feeling even more down.

I remember going through my own search for happiness in my days of suffering and once tried to get a friend to go on some weekend retreat with me. He said something that stopped me in my tracks' Paul you spend all your time talking about life and trying to improve yourself and I'll just get on with living it'. He wasn't being mean saying this, he just had no desire for all this self-improvement stuff and just felt the best way to enjoy life and be happy was just to go out and live it and not constantly work on himself. I never did go on that retreat!

The best way to be happy is not to try to suppress or get rid of any sadness but to fully allow its presence and let your mood change naturally. I don't mean wallow in it; I just mean allow its presence without trying to escape it, without identifying with it. Just see it as some inner experience that will pass.

I would rather feel happy than sad - everyone would - but I no longer resist it or try to change my experience. I don't turn to anything to get rid of or suppress any sadness that is around and the sadness no longer feels like a huge dark cloud; it just feels like an experience. Due to this, I can honestly say that I spend far less time feeling down than I used to do and when I do it has lost its potential to pull me down further as I don't label it as anything more than a passing mind state.

Obviously, if there are outside influences or your current circumstances making you unhappy and this is the real cause of your sadness, then you can make changes there but if we are talking about general moods and mind states that are out of your control, then just allow them to come and go without trying to manipulate them in any way.

I hope that helps.

Question: *Paul, my main problem is I can't seem to switch off from the subject. It's all I seem to think about morning till night. How can I begin to think of other things?*

This question comes up time and time again. The reason you can think of nothing else is because you keep feeding the subject of anxiety into your subconscious mind, be it through worrying, analysing and research. The subject just takes over your life and so the outside world starts to fade into the background. I am forever telling people how pointless and counterproductive all this, researching, obsessing and analysing is.

When I understood things, then I basically stepped out of my own pointless war and just went back to living. Instead of reading about anxiety, I would read about cycling. Instead of researching the subject, I would research holiday destinations. I dipped into the subject now and again, but that was it. It was no longer the sole focus of my life and now my mind had other things to think about it and so in time, my focus shifted naturally. I would still have the odd day when I felt I could think of nothing else, but I understood this was just the habit of previously thinking about myself and the subject still hanging around and the less I engaged in it, then the more the habit died down naturally.

It is like breaking up with an ex. Even after the break-up, you will have days when you can think of nothing else. However, as you start adding new things into your life and don't actively think about them, they become a distant memory and your focus naturally begins to shift towards other things. But, if all you do is think about them every day, look through old photo and letters while trying to analyse where it went wrong, then your focus will stay on the relationship and these thoughts will forever be in your mind.

If you want to stop thinking about the subject of anxiety, then allow your mind to do so if it wishes, which, through habit, it will for now. You can't stop thinking about something by trying not to, as the previous habit you have built will make sure the subject comes to the forefront of your mind for a while longer. But if you no longer feed the habit by consciously doing so, then the habit and your obsession with it will fade naturally.

It is a similar situation to when a person first leaves prison after many years of incarceration. At first, they will still think about their time in prison. Any attempt to do the opposite would not work as it is all they have known for years. But, once they go back to a normal life, the shift will begin naturally as they start to readjust and live in the outside world once again.

Engage in life and you will think about life, engage in the subject of anxiety and all you will think about is anxiety. The problem at the moment is that you are not having any breaks from the subject; it is what holds your attention and focus. You may have a constant running commentary on how you are feeling and how best to fix or manage it. It truly never ends for some.

Hopefully, the words in this book can eliminate so many of your concerns and the subject will just form a small part of your life as you begin to let go of the constant obsession you may be having with yourself and how you are feeling. If you need to read up on the subject or need a reminder, then that is fine as long as you then go back to living a life outside of yourself and the subject. Again, there is nothing wrong here. This state you find yourself in has been self-created by thinking of nothing else. When you start to shift your focus in a natural way, then you will have a variety of other things to think about and the subject will eventually fade into the background.

Question: *The thing that annoys me the most is that I know my fears are irrational, but they win every time and I end up hiding away and missing out on life. Why?*

I hid away for one reason and one reason only, and that was because I did not want to feel certain emotions, so the best way to not feel them was to hide away. Firstly, we need to ask ourselves if we fear the place or the situation we are going into, or the feelings that the place or situation may bring? The truth is, it is never the place or situation, as there truly is nothing to fear there. If there was, then everyone would experience the same anxieties and fears.

Fear is an illusion the mind creates. The world spins exactly the same for everyone. The only difference is that someone with anxiety may perceive it differently, but how they perceive it is not necessarily reality. The way we are tricked is that when we feel a certain fear in our mind, we automatically believe the cause of our fear to be outside of ourselves and this is why we then start to avoid places or certain situations. The trouble is, the more we avoid the situation/place where the fear arose, the stronger the mind relates that place to being a problem and so the fear response is turned up. Again, the system is working as it should. Through a process of avoidance, your mind now believes that there is danger in a situation that is perfectly harmless.

There is a well-known saying;

Feel the fear and do it anyway

All this saying really means, is that the fear response that has been triggered is a false alarm and so to turn this response down and teach your mind that you are perfectly safe, then you need to do it anyway with the energy of fear present. Your mind soon picks up that you are genuinely safe through a continued doing and so the fear response is eventually turned off.

Your mind's job is to remember and store things from past experiences so that it can protect you. If a dog attacks you at a particular house, then the next time you approach that house your mind goes into its memory bank and warns you to be careful and hence you will feel some fear. It is part of your mind's make-up to keep you safe and it actually believes it is doing you a favour, which in this case it is. But there are certain occasions when it goes into its memory bank and remembers the time when you felt anxious or avoided a certain experience and so it brings on the same response when there is no real danger or threat. If you then continue to avoid this place due to blindly following this fear response, your mind thinks it was right to feed you the warning and the response is then repeated. Due to your actions, it fully believes that it did its job correctly and will continue to protect you in these situations.

So even though the response was created due to your past behaviours, it has still got it wrong. It is firing off a warning when it is not needed, but you can't just tell it so. It doesn't grasp language as we know it. The only language it truly understands and follows is your actions, and if you keep confirming that it's right by running away or avoiding, then the reaction will never change.

You have to take your mind by the hand and teach it that it is wrong through the only language it understands, which is through non-avoidance, by overriding the fear response and working through wisdom and not an emotion. So, the next time you get the pang of fear, the only way to let it know that you're perfectly safe is to allow yourself to experience this response, see it through and no longer try to escape the situation you are in. By doing this, you are teaching your mind that there is no danger in this situation and so the fear response starts to be turned down and your life begins to open back up.

Yes, this approach means feeling the discomfort of fear, but you are more than capable of handling this. Fear is nothing more than an uncomfortable energy shift within the body, one that is utterly harmless and doesn't lead to you losing it. The more you allow yourself to experience it, the more apparent this becomes.

Fear also has its limits, but people never give themselves the chance to find this one important fact out. The first reaction, when faced with the feeling of fear, is to retreat and not experience its uncomfortable, but harmless, nature. My life did not open up because I found a way to eliminate fear. It is a hardwired response in all of us, so trying to eliminate it is an impossible task. My life opened up because I lost my fear of fear and lived my life, whether I felt it or not. My fear of this energy shift lessened and its presence hardly bothered me. I am not saying the feeling was not uncomfortable but getting my life back meant I was more than willing to allow its presence. Due to this, I no longer avoided any situation and so the fear response was turned right down and I was able to engage in life as I wished.

Question: You mention doing nothing a lot. Surely, I need to take some action?

Doing nothing does not mean lying around on the sofa all day doing nothing. In fact, I tell people to become more active, go back to following their hobbies and passions and start living again. Doing nothing points more towards what not to do, as anxiety sufferers are always stuck in 'doing' while trying to recover. I could ask a friend what he does about how he feels all day and he would say 'Nothing, what do you mean?' it does not mean he does nothing in his daily life; it just means he does not waste energy continually worrying while trying to monitor and fix himself.

If you look at someone who is healthy and does not suffer from anxiety, ask yourself what they do all day? They aren't obsessing about anything; they aren't constantly thinking about something; they aren't always worrying about something; they aren't in a constant battle with themselves all day. This is why they feel so much better. Just because you don't feel great doesn't mean you have to fall into all these rituals that create so much extra suffering.

Any suffering you feel is mainly due to these actions and not because you have been picked on by some outside force. It is not like getting the flu, where it is completely out of your control. This is why you can never recover through more doing, worrying, thinking or obsessing, as it is all this that is causing the suffering in the first place, so how could it ever lead to a cure? Surely the cure lies in no longer doing what is creating your suffering! This is such an important and obvious point that so many miss it.

So, doing nothing is just a pointer to no longer battling with yourself, as there truly is nothing to battle against. Healing will only come when you step out of your own way and cease this inner war. If your mind is tired and weary from all you have put it through, does it not make sense that the poor thing just needs you to stop and give it the rest it needs to heal itself?

Does it not make sense that if your nerves are shattered through worry, the fuel of worry must be cut off so they can heal? Does it not make sense that if your body is full of anxiety, attempting to suppress it while adding more anxiety through worry will never give you a chance to be free of it? Does it not make sense that if you are stuck in a constant loop of thinking about yourself, the answer is just to stop obsessing about how you feel and all things personal?

So, doing nothing basically means you stop creating the very suffering that you are trying to escape from.

The more control I let go of, the more control I felt I had. If you don't hook on to an emotion or a thought, then it will pass right on through, just as energy does. If you want that emotion or thought to hang around and grow by you adding more energy and fuel to it, then I suggest you try and deny it, argue with it, suppress it or run away from it. Do this and you will see what little control you have over trying to change any thought or emotion, apart from increasing it.

It was the same when I felt mentally off. Trying to change or deny the experience just made it worse. If I left my mind alone to do what it wanted, then the confusion passed far quicker and clarity returned. When any part of your body heals, then there is some pain and discomfort as it does so, this is how healing works. You are always far better falling into your suffering than trying to fight against it.

So again, doing nothing does not mean hiding away from life, which really means you are hiding away from feelings that certain situations or interactions may bring. If you want your life back, then you have to go and live it. If you want to build your confidence, then you need to mix again. The best way to recover is to live again, mix again, get out in nature, go back to the things that you enjoyed and follow your hobbies and passions. You can do all of these things, so don't let any emotions or old conditioned thoughts tell you otherwise. My life was on hold for many years because I fell for the big anxiety lie and hid away. My life became narrower and more restricted, my confidence plummeted and my social skills dropped alarmingly. I was no longer living; I was just existing.

To finish here is a question from my blog and a lady called Stephanie who I had previously helped replied in such a great way to her that I thought it was worth sharing.

How do you move to acceptance? I do have a core belief that anxiety is dangerous to me. I believe it will lead me to me having a "mental breakdown" or a place where I can't cope and so I try and stay on top of it all. I just need reassurance that the anxiety is not dangerous, I can handle it and that I won't be like this forever. These are my core concerns with my anxiety and why I can't seem to move forward. Any thoughts or help?

Char

Char, The problem with reassurance is it's short-lived. At first, you may feel better, but then the old fears creep in and you're back to trying to find that word, phrase or thing that comforts you. It is your current anxious state that is constantly needing reassurance, not you. So just leave all the questions and concerns unanswered, the more you involve yourself in reassuring the anxious mind, the more reassurance it will need.

Nolan has said on here many times that it was when he finally felt utterly hopeless and defeated that he started making progress. Why? Because he stopped trying to fix and manage his inner state and fully surrendered to how he felt, no matter how awful. He even accepted that he might feel this way forever. He was done looking for solutions, done trying to feel better, done looking for answers or reassurance; he just went back to living his life and took how he felt with him.

There will always be a new sensation or thought that will have you questioning once again. You have to decide that enough is enough. You're done trying to figure it all out. You're done trying to comfort and reassure yourself. If you're scared, fine, if your anxious, OK. But just let yourself fall into that place you most fear, the one you seek constant reassurance from and in doing so you may finally find there was nothing there to fear in the first place. This is when your need for reassurance will fall away naturally as you will realise there was nothing to fear in the first place; it was nothing but your mind's imagination.

Stephanie

Chapter 15

Living a Life Without Stress

As you will now have gathered, just about everyone reached their anxious state through too much worry and stress, basically pushing their body and mind beyond its limits. When we recover or are going through recovery, it is wise to take a good look at what brought you to initially seeking help. You won't get very far trying to recover while you continue to worry and stress about the same things that brought you to this point in the first place.

Even if the situation or situations that brought on the anxiety are still there, it is not a problem; you just need to learn to look at these things differently. As I said before, it is never your life situation that causes anxiety; it is your thoughts about it that does. When I hear friends and family stressing over little things, it seems so trivial to me now. I just sit back and see the old me and thank my lucky stars that I no longer fall into this worry trap. Going through what I did certainly changed me for the better and I don't regret it, otherwise; I would be joining in with them stressing and worrying about nothing in particular.

People are always commenting on how much calmer I seem these days, as though nothing seems to bother me. I don't purposely try to be this way, I just learnt so much about worry and stress that I don't go there anymore. Yes, bad things still happen, but then again, so do plenty of good things. I have learnt to see life as a balance of good and bad, isn't that how life works for everyone? I never complain when things go well, so why would I complain when they don't and what purpose would it serve apart from making me feel like crap for a while anyway?

If there is any part of your life that you can change to make it less stressful then do so, be it taking on less, cutting your hours down if you feel over-worked, learning to say no to others that burden you, going out more in nature and having more time for yourself. Take a good look at your life and see if there is room for change or things that could improve it. I explained in my last book how exercise and a better diet helped me and I followed this through with a complete lifestyle change. I still carry on looking after myself to this day. I am not perfect by any means, but I now understand how looking after yourself better and getting a good night's rest is vital to your overall well-being.

Searching for happiness

A lot of people search for happiness in outside things. Yet when they get the big car and the new house and that feeling of emptiness is still there, they think: 'Well I have everything so it must be me' and so then turn to self-help looking for a solution. This is why the self-help industry is booming. I learnt that the best way to be happy is to get the inside right then everything else falls into place. I regularly tell people that they are looking for happiness in the wrong place. If you feel lost and miserable and look for someone else or some possession to make you happy, it won't work. That is not where true happiness and peace lie.

I live a much simpler life these days and realise what is important; following my true passions, helping others and spending time with those closest to me. I got rid of all the negative and toxic people in my life and don't even watch the news anymore, as I began to see that 90% of it was negative or scaremongering.

After my recovery, I really went off drinking alcohol and that was pretty much what my old social life consisted of. But I no longer wanted to go down that road and knew I had to make changes. I grew tired of hangovers and wasted days and wanted to follow what made me happy. I knew that my priorities had shifted and what used to make me happy no longer did. So, I joined a Buddhist class, a walking group, joined a gym and bought myself a bicycle. Due to all these changes, I live a far more fulfilling life now and it feels more in line with what I want.

We can't all pack our jobs in and move to a vineyard in France, but we can all make some changes that will help us to lead a happier and more stress-free life, even if that means just having a new attitude towards it. If we could just learn to no longer take life so seriously, to just let it all unfold as it does with all the good and bad days that may come along. Learn to appreciate what you do have instead of what you don't have. Sometimes all you need is a new attitude and a new perception on life and it all appears different, friendlier and less hostile, something to enjoy and not constantly worry about.

So much anxiety is created through inner conflict, for example: 'I want to achieve more, be happier, richer, prettier, younger. If only my partner would be more like this, if only others would be kinder, then I would be OK.' When you are in constant conflict with life and with what is, then all you do is create stress and suffering. When we let life play out as it does, then we find we are happier, more at peace and achieve more naturally. It is not a forced peace or happiness, and you don't have to go outside yourself to find it. When we start appreciating what we do have and not what we don't, then life gets so much easier. It is the constant need for more that creates the discomfort and unhappiness. I have to blame the media for a lot of this, that and a consumer market that will never point us to the true source of contentment.

I once saw a program about people in Africa where some children were playing football with a sock bound by tape and they did not have a care in the world. They were kicking it around and really enjoying themselves. Then one of the women gave them a pencil each and their faces lit up. Seeing that had a profound effect on me. It showed me that they did not see what was lacking in their life; they just really appreciated what they did have. They weren't living a life always wanting more; they simply accepted each moment as it was.

Change is not always easy, as plodding along feels easier at times, but nothing is gained from this. If you want things to change, then you are the only one responsible for making it happen and trust me the rewards are so worth it. But even just a change in attitude towards life can have a real impact on your well-being.

Chapter 16

Summing Up

Anxiety was never the true cause of my problems; it was the ensuing battle with it, that caused the real suffering.

After reading this book, you will now know that it was not written to give you a bunch of techniques or rules to follow because you don't need them. Recovery comes through an understanding of how you have been keeping yourself in the cycle of suffering, and a certain amount of courage to face what you have been avoiding and suppressing for so long.

So many people come to me for help and because I can't give them an instant answer (that doesn't exist) on how to rid themselves of their suffering, they go off searching elsewhere, only to eventually find out that it is a fruitless pursuit. But you have to allow people to find out the truth for themselves. When they have had enough of searching and have got nowhere with all their strategies and techniques, they will eventually start to look in another direction.

The real aim of this book is to finally end the struggle you are having with yourself so that you no longer stay in a loop of recreating your suffering. I also hope to educate you enough so that your focus of attention is taken away from the subject of you and put it fully back on life. You were not put on this planet to work on yourself for the rest of your life; you were put here to accept yourself as you are. You were also not put on here to avoid life; you were put here to fully experience it.

All I am trying to do is point you towards the truth so that you can see it for yourself. When you see something for yourself and really understand the message in these words, then the struggle you have been having with yourself starts to fall away automatically. You cannot 'try' not to struggle, as this can end up being a struggle in itself. The end of struggling comes through understanding, by seeing how much suffering that struggle was creating.

Where recovery is concerned, knowledge really is the key to everything. Even to this day, I continue with my research and never tire of learning more about suffering and how the mind and body works and responds. I never stop learning because I want to be able to give the best advice I can. Recovery does not come through struggle; it comes through seeing something. When you truly see something, then it makes no sense to carry on doing what was hurting you. Understanding can eliminate so much suffering.

This is why I go into detail about a lot of the symptoms and explain the reason for them. It is why I talk about neural pathways, mental exhaustion and thoughts. I understand that you can't just tell someone to allow themselves to feel how they do and that's the end of it. They need to truly understand why they feel like they do and what is keeping them in the cycle before they trust in this process. Understanding also takes the edge of how you are feeling, it takes the fear away from a lot of the symptoms you are experiencing and so you are then more able to allow their presence and live alongside them.

The peace you are looking for lies behind everything you have fought against, everything you have tried to run away from or suppressed. You need to take away your resistance and allow your emotions to be felt as they are without trying to push them away, without trying to distract yourself or change them; even the ones that cause you real discomfort. Your body is doing nothing more than bringing them up to be released, to free them up from your inner space and if you want to be free of them, then you have to be willing to experience them.

It is the same with an exhausted mind; you don't try to fix it. Any exhaustion/discomfort you currently feel was caused by your past attempts at constantly trying to fix yourself; you mentally wore yourself out. When you stop doing this, then the exhausted mind finally gets the chance it needs to heal.

So, as you should now see, no longer doing anything replenishes so much mental energy and helps to release all the anxious/fearful energy inside of you. Not only that, but it also helps to put your attention back onto the world outside of you as you are no longer spending all your waking hours obsessing about your inner world and so you feel far more engaged with your surroundings. None of this is complicated when you really see it.

The length of time it takes for real progress to occur is different for everyone and can depend on the length of time you have suffered and how much you have suppressed in the past. When I read people's stories of recovery through the blog or in an email, it is usually a few months after they first came to me for help that they talk of real change. The reason I mention this is so that people don't fall into the trap of being impatient.

We all have a desire to get where we want to be right now or as soon as possible, but it is that constant struggle to achieve this that works against us and takes us in the opposite direction. When you feel an urgency to be somewhere else, you are pushing hard against where you are right now. When you are more accepting of where you are, then you naturally fall back to where you need to be. Time is your healer here, not your enemy.

I really try to get across to people that there is no battle to fight and no enemy to defeat. I have spoken to so many people who have recovered who can now clearly see what they previously did wrong. They can't believe what they used to put themselves through on a daily basis and how they ever thought it could be the answer to freedom.

Even when things start to click and you feel more at ease and you begin to see where you have gone wrong, you will still feel remnants of your past struggles. You can be left with a lot of trapped anxiety and emotions that still need to be felt and released, your mind may still be exhausted through years of mental effort and struggle, and you may still have a lot of old conditioned thoughts to see through.

Trust me, none of this is important and is just past suffering that needs time to heal. During my recovery, I had to go through many cycles. There were some days of real suffering and some days of pure bliss; days where my mind was racing and noisy and days where it felt calm and settled; but I fully accepted that it was a process I had to go through.

The best advice I can give to anyone is that it is never about trying to constantly feel good; it is about accepting yourself as you are, whatever that current experience may be. This is what will finally bring peace within. The rules of nature tell us that everything balances out when left alone. We are no different as we are all part of nature.

You don't have to go on a long self-help road to get back to who you truly are; all you really need is a better understanding. In my case, a simple realisation could wipe out years of misunderstanding and take away so much suffering. My words here are meant to give you that understanding, to awaken something in you, so you see the truth for yourself and end this constant war you are having with yourself.

Good luck with rediscovering your true nature and regaining your life.

Paul David

More from Paul David

If you would like further reading to complement this book, my first book *At Last a Life* can be ordered through any UK bookshop, my website or Amazon and is also available on the kindle. It is also now available in Audiobook form to download from my website.

If you would like to keep up to date with me on social media, then you can find me on Facebook at www.facebook.com/anxietynomoreuk or you can follow me on twitter @anxietynomoreuk